Active Learning in Graduate Education

Listening, curiosity and love

This work was supported by FAPERJ, the Rio de Janeiro State funding agency for research, with a Research Project Grant, through "Young Scientist of Our State" Program E-26/201.356/2021 (Brazil).

This work was supported by FCT, I.P., the Portuguese national funding agency for science, research and technology, under the Project UIDB/04521/2020 (Portugal).

Active Learning in Graduate Education

Listening, curiosity and love

Ana Paula André
Cláucia Piccoli Faganello (Ed)
Igor Vinicius Lima Valentim (Ed)
Kelly Cebelia das Chagas do Amaral
Najara Escarião Agripino
Paulo de Tarso Xavier Sousa Júnior

ComPassos Coletivos
2023

ComPassos Coletivos

livros@compassoscoletivos.com.br

Rio de Janeiro | Brazil

Editorial Board

Profª. Drª. Daniele Maria Oliveira de Jesus (Australia)
Prof. Dr. Igor Vinicius Lima Valentim (Brazil)
Prof. Dr. José Maria Carvalho Ferreira (Portugal)
Prof. Dr. Paulo Roberto da Silva (Brazil)
Prof. Dr. Ricardo Luiz Pereira Bueno (Brazil)
Profª. Drª. Simone Torres Evangelista (Brazil)

© 2023 by The Authors

Original Title: *Metodologias Ativas na Pós-Graduação: escuta, curiosidade e amor*

Translated from Portuguese by Igor Vinicius Lima Valentim and Cláucia Piccoli Faganello

First edition: September 2023

Cover Art and Image: Igor Vinicius Lima Valentim
Backcover: image from Bing Han at Unsplash.com

Excerpts from this book may be copied, shared and/or reproduced, as long as you give appropriate credit and the source is cited. You may not use this material for commercial purposes. To reproduce the complete book, authorization from the publisher is required.

Catalog in Publication

A593

Active Learning in Graduate Education: listening, curiosity and love / Edited by Igor Vinicius Lima Valentim and Cláucia Piccoli Faganello. - Rio de Janeiro: ComPassos Coletivos, 2023.

152 p.

Includes references, index and information about the authors.

ISBN (print): 978-85-663980-5-2
ISBN (digital EPUB): 978-85-663980-6-9

1. Higher Education 2. University 3. Graduate Education 4. Educational Practices 5. Active Methods I. Title.

CDU 37.022

To Elza and Genaro,
eternal references

CONTENTS

13 For a Graduate Education based on listening, curiosity, and love
Igor Vinicius Lima Valentim

29 Encompassing voices: how was the experience of attending the course Listening, Curiosity and Love?
Ana Paula André, Kelly Cebelia, Cláucia Faganello, Paulo de Tarso e Najara Escarião

35 Is a more loving Administration science possible?
Cláucia Piccoli Faganello

59 Curious Amora: looking for new forms of teaching and learning
Kelly Cebelia das Chagas do Amaral

73 Memories and pandemic diasporas: learnings and a short film
Paulo de Tarso Xavier Sousa Junior

87 Dialogues with teachers: technology and continuing teacher education
Ana Paula André

103 Listening in academic processes: supervisor/supervisee relationship in Graduate Education
Najara Escarião Agripino

127 Considerations on the construction of this tool-book
Igor Vinicius Lima Valentim

133 Index

143 About the authors

1

For a Graduate Education based on listening, curiosity, and love

Igor Vinicius Lima Valentim

How can we stimulate the construction of a society that is more open to listening, that values people's curiosities, and that has more loving interpersonal relationships? How can public universities, more specifically Graduate Education, contribute to this direction?

To present this work I need first to present the context in which it was written. This book is born of the richness and power of encounters. And the encounters we have in our lives don't always take place in person.

What readers find here is the result of a collective experimentation-adventure that began in a Graduate course called **Listening, curiosity, and love**, for Master's and Doctoral students. It was taught in 2022, from the Graduate Program in History of Sciences, Techniques and Epistemology, of the Federal University of Rio de Janeiro (UFRJ[1]), Brazil, in synchronous remote mode and totally based on active learning methods.

The class had Master's and PhD students from all five regions of Brazil. There were more than 120 applicants, of which (unfortunately) I could only select approximately 50 to start the semester.

Listening, curiosity, and love? But what Graduate course is this?

---

[1] UFRJ is a Brazilian public university with 4,300+ tenured professors, 53,000+ undergraduate and 15,000+ graduate students (in 2023).

> **"How, from listening
> and openness to others,
> can we imagine and build
> other universities and other worlds?"**

This was the main motto for the creation of the course and its first offering.

This book focuses on what was produced, experienced, and lived. For this reason, it is not the ideal space for a thorough, detailed, and step-by-step explanation of the course itself. All its planning, methods, procedures, reflections, and educational perspectives are presented in another work[2].

Still, it is important, for the presentation of this book, to explain some aspects. **Listening, curiosity, and love** was based on three characteristics:

i. It was taught remotely, online, synchronously, and had applications open for students of any Graduate Program (GP) in Brazil, from any knowledge field or university, completely free of any kind of tuition or payment;

ii. It was entirely based on active learning methods, and designed with a transdisciplinary perspective, which placed the students' interests, curiosities, and the activities they produced at the center of the educational processes;

iii. It looked to stimulate the use of listening, curiosity, and the development of more loving interpersonal relationships.

---

[2] Valentim, 2024, in press.

i. A remote Graduate course in 2022?

In 2020 and 2021, with the covid-19 pandemic at its peak, most Brazilian public universities shifted their undergraduate and graduate courses to remote/online mode. It wasn't easy, but I decided that, still in 2022, **Listening, curiosity, and love** would be taught remotely since its very first edition. And not only that: the course would be open to Master's and PhD students of any Graduate Program in Brazil, without charging absolutely any fees to students[3].

There were numerous challenges, including from an institutional standpoint (from norms to conservative colleagues). The university (UFRJ) did not have a clear policy on the possibility of Graduate courses being taught in remote or even hybrid mode. In addition, even today, in 2023, it still does not have an integrated academic system through which students from other institutions that want to take its Graduate courses can register and request enrollment in the desired disciplines each semester.

Besides, even with all the technological advancement available, there are still no integrated institutional records of students from other universities who attend the courses offered by the more than 130 UFRJ's Graduate Programs. Putting it clearly, the registrations of these students are made

---

[3] In Brazil, there is no tuition in any of the Master's and PhDs in public universities. Although, there are some universities that, even though they are public, charge fees to Master's and PhD students from other universities (although also public) to attend their Graduate courses. Today, in 2023, the Federal University of Minas Gerais (UFMG) is an example of this, charging BRL 194.57 per course. You can read more details about this (in Portuguese) on: https://www2.ufmg.br/drca/drca/Home/Pos-Graduacao/Disciplina-Isolada/Disciplina-Isolada-2023-11.

directly by each Program in isolation, keeping precarious controls in spreadsheets or something similar.

The more than 120 applications we received to the 2022 edition of **Listening, curiosity, and love** by Master's and PhD students from other universities were processed manually by our Graduate Program, demanding a huge amount of work from the Secretariat and myself.

Students from other universities who have taken **Listening, curiosity, and love** and who were approved at the end of the semester received an official declaration so they could validate the credit hours with their Graduate Programs of origin. This document was issued after a Herculean and manual work of the secretariat of our Program, based on a list I manually elaborated.

There is an even more serious and worrying aspect beyond all this manual, Herculean and inefficient work: the lack of institutional knowledge about what a public university with more than a century of existence does. Today, a year later, if the Dean - or any of UFRJ's administrators or faculty - wishes to analyze how many (or which) students took part in the university's Graduate courses in 2022, it will only "see" the internal students of UFRJ itself.

Incredibly, while other universities in Brazil, such as the State University of Campinas (UNICAMP), have solid academic registration systems that allow the electronic application, enrollment, grading, and certification of "external" or "special" students (from other universities), at UFRJ these external students are almost invisible.

In official terms, the 2022 class of **Listening, curiosity, and love** had only ten UFRJ students, according to the institution's academic system. I, as a professor, in the same system, worked only for these ten students. Meanwhile, all the other more than 40 students – from other universities – who were selected to attend (and effectively did), among the more than 120 applicants, were and continue to be absolutely invisible to the institution. This is invisible, almost clandestine work. Invisible social impact. Invisible outreach. UFRJ does not fully recognize faculty work or its social impact as an educational institution beyond its internal students. The university does not know who it serves, its size, and value when it comes to the students of other institutions that take its courses each and every semester. A complete and absurd lack of knowledge and a waste of its effective work as a public university.

Fortunately, even in a complex institutional context, the coordination of our Graduate Program showed solidarity and supported the project. In the end, the university, more broadly, turned a blind eye to the professors who offered graduate courses in synchronous remote mode in 2022 (and still in 2023).

Many people are quick to say that higher education, in remote mode, harms concrete participation, since there is no physical presence and, supposedly, no involvement, dedication, or exchange. This can happen in some specific cases, as with the use of traditional methods or when pre-recorded contents, pre-prepared materials, and pre-determined activities are the courses' basis. In these cases,

I could agree that there would be a higher possibility of a poorer and more limited experience. However, when we are discussing the universe of Master's and PhD courses, this is not the rule when:

1. remote mode is used in conjunction with active learning methods;

2. there is a continuous and thorough incentive (and monitoring and rewarding) for students to produce authorial knowledge and develop creative activities;

3. the course is designed and built based on the students' interests and curiosities, articulating theoretical contents with research (and even fieldwork) activities.

Deciding that the course would be offered remotely, online, and synchronously, was no mere whim. Remote mode was chosen to foster the richness of having in the same class students from all over the national territory, providing opportunities for people from the most diverse cities of a continental country like Brazil to engage in a course because of their interest in its subject, and not only due to geographical proximity. And at no cost.

There was an immense desire to enhance the learning potential of the course's meetings, stimulating everybody to build and learn together, people from various locations, distinct areas of knowledge, and life histories, but with thematic interests that intersected in a transdisciplinary way. Valuing the power of diversity and encounters! Inclusion, outreach, collective construction, and potential richness are derived from a strong diversity altogether.

ii. Active learning methods in a Graduate course

Listening, curiosity, and love used active learning methods, which looked to put the interest and dedication of students at the center of the educational processes. There were no traditional lectures. The live meetings over the internet were spaces for debates, exchanges, horizontal dialogues, and collective learning. And for these meetings to work in a powerful way, we needed to reinforce the importance of preparation moments outside the classes' specific hours, in which each student should not only read proposed texts but also produce writings, participate in the collective elaboration of the references of the discipline itself, criticize the work of the other classmates and develop an individual project throughout the semester.

The use of active learning methods made the discipline, from its start, "hands-on" and demanded much more work both from the teacher and the students. As stated above, in addition to the readings, already traditional in Master's and PhD courses, the students had to produce several activities throughout the semester and, from the first meeting, began to build a final individual authorial work of a theme freely chose by each of them, that should be linked to their interests and curiosities. This final work was the main component through which the students would be evaluated (and graded, since there were no exams) and required:

- the inclusion of a listening component, demanding the students to listen to another person(s);
- to be based on a curiosity, a doubt, or something that the students did not know and wanted to investigate. Or that they knew little and wanted to know more. The theme was free but could not be based on the "showing" of something they already knew beforehand;
- to be focused on proposing changes for the construction of more loving relationships and/or worlds.

The course sought to stimulate that listening, curiosity, and love **were not only discussed and debated topics from texts, films, and other materials, but that, in addition, they were also experienced by everyone throughout the course**.

The final work of each student was progressively built. It was presented, commented, and criticized by all the attendants at three separate times during the semester. Collective learning was strengthened, and we looked to escape from a logic based exclusively on a result to also value the processes that led to the "finished" product. What mattered the most was not only the finished product at the end of the course, but also its development stages. Thus, the very construction process of the final work, with its various difficulties, was able to be a source of collective learning. Therefore, it was not a question of arriving at a single right answer (because there would not be any), nor of producing something that would be evaluated only by a teacher.

If, on the one hand, a course with this design demanded much more work and dedication than a traditional one, on the other hand, it put this heavy work at the service of the students' curiosities and interests. Everybody worked harder, yes, but towards the construction of something that could make sense to them, that was chosen by them.

The combination of remote, online, and synchronous mode, with the fact that the course was based on active learning methods, has increased the possibility of exchanges, encounters, and bridges. We expanded the outreach of a public university beyond its physical walls, increasing the quality of its education with the use of active learning methods, fostering collective knowledge construction between students from the most diverse regions of Brazil and from quite different areas of knowledge.

iii. For relationships with more love, please

It is important to emphasize that this book does not seek to construct generalizations or prescriptions about better or worse ways of constructing graduate education. Academia is an extremely conservative space, in Brazil and globally. In the sphere of interpersonal relationships there is idolatry, cliques, followers, vanities, favoritism, violence, harassment[4,5,6], pimping[7], among many other aspects. Learning is often self-centered and disconnected from the world. It is still exceedingly rare, in 2023, to find courses in which the interests and curiosities of students are not only respected, but mainly placed at the center of what is developed.

It is important to complain and denounce, but it is not enough. Here, we focus on what we have collectively built to propose and share alternatives, resistances, spaces of joy and serious work.

At the same time, it is necessary to warn readers: this book presents no "best way" about teaching in graduate school, but only experimentations and openness to different possibilities. We wanted to stimulate different forms of learning in Master's and PhDs from a Brazilian public university. These experimentations and possibilities were handmade with one thing in mind: towards worlds with more listening, more curiosity, and love.

---

[4] VALENTIM, I. V. L. Cafetinagem Acadêmica: Alguém tem medo de pesquisar as relações acadêmicas? Polêmica, v. 16, n. 3, p. 19–36, 24 ago. 2016. DOI: 10.12957/polemica.2016.25200.

[5] VALENTIM, I. V. L. Between academic pimping and moral harassment in higher education: An autoethnography in a Brazilian public university. Journal of Academic Ethics, v. 16, n. 2, p. 151–171, 2018. DOI: 10.1007/s10805-018-9300-y.

[6] VALENTIM, I. V. L. Entre naturalizações e desassossegos: educando para tolerar o intolerável? Revista on line de Política e Gestão Educacional, p. 265–279, 2018. DOI: 10.22633/rpge.v22.nesp1.2018.10794.

[7] VALENTIM, I. V. L. Cafetinagem acadêmica, assédio moral e autoetnografia. Rio de Janeiro: Compassos Coletivos, 2022. DOI: 10.5281/zenodo.7048194.

Propositional resistance: building alternatives is never easy

Higher education is still often medieval. Both in methods and interpersonal relationships. The educational methods used in most of Master's and Doctoral courses in Brazil are usually based on the idea that knowledge can be 'transmitted' and the consequent treatment of students as ignorant, as Paulo Freire warned[8] decades ago.

Students are still considered, by many, people devoid of knowledge and who are in the university so that the professors can 'pass' knowledge in the best possible way to illuminate them. This is a very widespread standpoint, both among students and faculty. We need to be aware: the methods used daily in undergraduate and graduate classes say a lot about the way we see and feel the world, relationships, education and, ultimately, about our values and subjectivities.

We complain about students' disinterest in higher education settings, and this is apparent in many situations. But we also need to look at what we, as faculty, do with their interests and curiosities. We must seek to understand (and criticize) our own attitudes and to question our own beliefs. Is it critical to put the curiosity and interest of students at the center of the educational processes? Yes, and being clear that this will demand a lot more work for everyone involved..

Technology-mediated teaching is common.

---

[8] FREIRE, P. Pedagogia do oprimido. Rio de Janeiro: Paz e Terra, 2002.

Experiences with active learning methods are more easily found at the undergraduate level[9]. But there is still a clear lack of **Graduate courses (Master's and PhDs) taught in synchronous remote mode that are, at the same time, entirely based on active learning methods**.

Even in 100% face-to-face classes there have always been (and will continue to be) people (students and teachers) with low commitment, involvement, and participation: without the expected dedication. There have always been people whose physical presence in the classroom was questionable, since they could be found immersed in side conversations, physical or electronic distractions, corridors, and/or other activities in no way related to the moment of face-to-face classes.

How about we openly discuss about what we live inside our classrooms, instead of using a hypocritical nostalgia that pretends as if everything is wonderful in in-person higher education?

How about we discuss more about the potential and pitfalls of using remote classes in Graduate level courses with Master's and Doctoral students?

What I want to point out is that when we should desire to build a Graduate Education that is more focused on the interests and curiosities of students, we will need to pay attention not only to if the course is taught in-person, hybrid or remotely, but also to the learning methods we

---

[9] VALENTIM, I. V. L.; MOREIRA, M. M.; GONÇALVES, S. de O. dos S. Metodologias ativas no ensino remoto: uma autoetnografia. Rio de Janeiro: Compassos Coletivos, 2021.

use, the way courses are designed, planned and developed, what kind of creations will be developed by the students, what values will be stimulated by our attitudes, among other aspects. Some questions we can ask ourselves in this regard are (but are not limited to):

- → Do we request and reward students' authorial productions focused on their interest and curiosity?
- → Do the productions, works and activities throughout the semester value the autonomy and creativity of students?
- → What happens during the live meetings/classes? Are they used for merely expository moments that could be done in other locations?
- → Do the products made by students value their authorship, production, and creativity, or do we expect them to be mere repeaters of theories and concepts?
- → Is there an effort to have some connection to the students' dreams and desires? Is there an effort to connect with society in more general terms, outside the university?
- → Are there stimuli for the development of works that articulate teaching, research, experiences, and even fieldwork?

Higher Education institutions are extremely conservative because most of their members are extremely conservative. Simple as that. And conservatism is present not in the contents that are taught or researched, but in the attitudes of everyday life, in the little things thrown under the rug, in the daily hypocrisies, that is, in the way each and every one builds interpersonal relationships, with all the intersections that exist between them: of power, pedagogical, work, study, among many others.

Building a Graduate Education that is open enough to allow the possibility of remote courses is not synonymous with ease when active learning methods are used, and students need to produce authorial activities and knowledge. There is no loss of quality, no massification. Quite the opposite. Classes need to have less students. And there is greater richness, diversity, and quality, with more demanded work and dedication needed.

Educational methods have never been, are not and never will be the silver bullet, the magic solution to all (higher) educational problems. Far from it. However, when active learning methods are used, combined with synchronous remote teaching, and with activities based on the interests and desires of students, Graduate level education may, perhaps, with some optimism, have some breath of hope in helping them build dreams of their own and no longer treat Master's and PhD students as unpaid employees of faculty or as mere repeaters of theories and methods. And that will take a lot more work, both for students and faculty. At the same time, it may increase meaning, energy, social commitment and, above all, joy.

2

Encompassing voices:
how was the experience of attending the course Listening, Curiosity and Love?

Ana Paula André
Kelly Cebelia
Cláucia Faganello
Najara Escarião
Paulo de Tarso

Ana Paula, Kelly Cebelia, Cláucia Faganello, Najara Escarião & Paulo de Tarso

We are still immersed in many transpandemic issues, and the academic space has become increasingly arduous and excluding in the face of some challenges that still arise. However, not everything in life is about bitterness: some moments will have sweet meanings. This perspective ended up uniting different, singular, and plural people in a university space that transgresses the logic of teaching and that aims to build an affective, inclusive, and empathetic education. This is how the authors of this book came together, through the conversion of our curiosities into an academic Graduate course offered in a remote format to master's and doctoral-level students from different parts of Brazil.

It was an innovative experience that may have initially provoked a certain strangeness due to its methodological form, giving students autonomy and instigating them to build their own knowledge. The space became an environment for reflection and self-knowledge, the exchange of experiences, breaking paradigms and building friendships that last beyond the discipline.

At first, when we heard Professor Igor Valentim's proposal, we couldn't help but ask ourselves: how should we start? How could this experience happen? Is it even possible for this to work out in the end?

Something totally new for the academic reality was presented to us: a mixture of freedom and at the same time insecurity. How could knowledge be collectively built from such diverse thoughts and experiences? The challenge of collectiveness (something belongs to several people) was presented from the very first moment: from the collaborative construction of the course's references through the conduction of classes, it was all openly discussed by the professor with all the students. This became an environment for self-reflection, in which we were encouraged to reflect on our individual and collective trajectories and experiences with Graduate studies so far. At the same time, we questioned ourselves about the university we would like to have and how to promote its construction. This became the starting point. Now we could set sail that anchor and brave that ocean!

We believe that everyone who arrived here was driven by curiosity, which is present in the course's title and provokes the actions that move us in search of the new. After all, what would be a Graduate course that is willing to truly listen? What part of the curiosities of all the people present in the classroom (even if virtual) could be converted into collective learning? And the most challenging, how to promote academic spaces and a more loving world?

Well, readers, feel invited to tour with us about this experience!

Some students saw the banner with the course's announcement and open call for applications on social media, others received it by email, WhatsApp groups and, still, some were invited because they were part of the Graduate program that offered it. Most of us did not know Professor Igor Valentim, the mentor in this process and the course's creator.

The course can also be called a "challenge". With many interested students at the beginning, some dropped out during the semester and others, moved by this challenge, stayed, and together resized their expectations. Breaking down the concept of an academic Graduate course has allowed us to build new possibilities and to take a different look at the construction of knowledge, listening and love in the educational field.

The experience we lived helped us bring a greater understanding of the educational process - regarding issues of affectivity and how much we can advance when we are instigated to participate in a concrete way - to our daily practice, considering that we are educators.

This experience left, in addition to learning and sharing with everyone involved, a sweet taste of nostalgia, affectionate memories, building bonds and friendships, talking and listening, but also the desire to continue the journey and flood other memories. with what takes us on a permanent journey: learning.

The group that writes these texts for you is part of the selected ones who felt challenged to continue with its purpose even after the formal course ended. We chose to continue with the work built in the course to take it to the world because, in order to build a new world, we need to dialogue with those who seek the same as us. This book is a fruit of that desire to share.

We are teachers and graduate students who work in different disciplines and in different Brazilian states. You will be able to taste our very diverse work propositions, which make this book a wealth of diversity. So, from north to south of this huge country called Brazil, we keep going, happy to know that geographically we may be far away, but the little seed of hope reconnects us and makes us believe that in our workspaces we are capable of applying what we have learned in a more affective and truly effective way, having a real formative sense.

In this course many paradigms related to academic rigidity were overcome and the contents' scientificity was always present in a more organic and fluid way. The knowledge built here will certainly remain after the course and its learnings will be taken to the LIFE that does not fit in our CVs and applied in daily life through our teaching practice, according to what each of us believes. A loving, respectful and educational teaching practice!

Well, we are happy and excited to share with you all our ideas, studies and, above all, affections. May these words come to you like a compass to navigate your own ocean. Who knows who we might end up meeting on this journey. We'll have a lot of curiosities, and we'll have a lot of affection left. We are waiting for you there!

A fraternal hug from Ana Paula, Kelly Cebelia, Cláucia Faganello, Najara Escarião and Paulo de Tarso.

3

Is a more loving Administration Science possible?

Cláucia Piccoli Faganello

Abstract

This chapter was built from the proposal to respond to a curiosity. This curiosity, about the field of knowledge in which I am inserted, generated the following research question: Is a more loving Administration Science possible? Based on this questioning and having Paulo Freire, Dassayeve Távora Lima, bell hooks, and Heribaldo Maia as a theoretical basis, the present work aims to: identify, through listening to people who make up this field, how they understand the Administration Science today and what they believe can change to make it more loving and welcoming. To this end, a case study was conducted, using a focus group as the data collection instrument (listening), along with the use of a tool where participants could anonymously provide observations on an online board. As research excerpt, master's and doctoral students of Administration from a Graduate Program in Administration at a Community University were invited. From the listening, it is possible to infer Administration can be a more loving science, but that depends on us and the structures being open to listening to what students have to say and being willing to think about a graduate course different from what we have today.

Introduction

Administration as a science is a controversial space. People usually choose this undergraduate course when they don't know very well what course they want to do. Very few people go into Administration because they want to be managers. Graduate studies are a little different, as in addition to Administration undergraduates, we also find students from other fields of study seeking a Master's or Doctorate degree, making the environment much more diverse and rich. Even so, there is dissatisfaction on the part of graduate students who find it difficult to carry out and complete their studies.

The reports are very diverse: from a lack of economic conditions to stay in the graduate school in such an unequal country to a lack of knowledge on conducting research and writing a dissertation or thesis. However, what we hear less is how fantastic, rewarding, and beneficial to people the graduate experience is. We usually hear this only after a graduate course completion, from those who overcome all barriers and typically say that graduate school is difficult but, ultimately, it is worth it.

This problem generated the curiosity to understand: is a more loving Administration science possible? Based on this question and with a focus on narrative methodologies, a project was proposed to identify, from listening to people who make up the field of scientific training in Administration, how they understand the science of Administration today and what they believe can change to make it more loving and welcoming.

Based on the discussion, this work is structured from an inductive, interactive, and recurrent process, aiming to understand the phenomenon of graduate science in Administration through a qualitative study designed in the form of a case study, having as a collection technique of narrative data the development of a focus group, which provided the opportunity to listen to five graduate students in Administration from a graduate program at a Community University in Rio Grande do Sul (RS), Brazil, comprising four Ph.D. students and one Master's degree student.

Inspiring theoretical basis

The questioning that guided this work arises from the concerns stemming from readings on neoliberalism, knowledge production, and from the belief in knowledge as a transforming tool and education as a path that still presents movements that question the structural logic taken as / considered hegemonic.

To think about knowledge production more lovingly, one must understand there are structures that act on the knowledge production system and on the University, making this process more challenging.

The neoliberal economic and political system is considered hegemonic worldwide, being defined as:

> [...] the theoretical principle and the doxa of a new form of State action, which is oriented not only to the maintenance of public order in a territory and

to the unification of a national market, but also to the construction of a world market and the active participation in the competition it imposes[1].

Therefore, neoliberalism is understood as a new form of State action that influences the functioning dynamics of all spheres of social life, being: "a mode of production of subjectivities, governmentality of bodies and management of psychic suffering, going beyond a purely economic way"[2]. Furthermore, neoliberalism raises the role of a symbolic power, as described by Bourdieu as an: "almost magic power that allows obtaining the equivalent of what is obtained by force (physical or economic), thanks to the specific mobilization effect"[3]. The objective world affects the "structured structures" that act as language, culture, discourses, and behaviors and present themselves through "instruments of domination" that determine how the division of physical and ideological work will occur[4].

From this understanding, it is necessary to "[...] understand how neoliberal logic colonized and radically modified not only universities and other academic spaces but also the training experience itself"[5]. The way knowledge is produced is intertwined with neoliberal precepts and beliefs. Therefore, doing things differently also implies breaking with

---

[1] LAVAL, C. Foucault, Bourdieu e a questão neoliberal. São Paulo: Elefante, 2020. Author's translation.

[2] LIMA, D. T. Prefácio. In: Neoliberalismo e sofrimento psíquico: o mal-estar nas universidades. Recife: Ruptura, 2022, p. 9. Author's translation.

[3] BOURDIEU, P. O poder simbólico. 7. ed. Rio de Janeiro: Bertrand Brasil, 2007, p. 14. Author's translation.

[4] Idem, p. 16.

[5] LIMA, D. T. Prefácio. In: Neoliberalismo e sofrimento psíquico: o mal-estar nas universidades. Recife: Ruptura, 2022, p. 11. Author's translation.

the hegemonic and dominant position, in which meritocracy is placed as if it were the only element that guarantees the success or the failure of a graduate student[6].

In this regard, bell hooks brings important elements to think about the problem constructively, as she says:

> When we point out the problem, when we express our complaint without a constructive focus on resolution, we take hope away. In this way, criticism can become just an expression of deep cynicism, which ends up supporting the dominant culture[7].

Thus, starting from a pedagogy inspired by Paulo Freire, bell hooks proposes that teaching, the production of knowledge, be always transgressive of our time, having the ability to challenge the existing logic to create resistance:

> [...] this ability to always start, to do, to rebuild, not to surrender, to refuse to mentally bureaucratize, to understand and live life as a process, as becoming, is something that has always accompanied me over the years[8].

In this space of resistance, of constant refusal, the proposal for more loving, healthy, and suitable environments for knowledge production is not a grinder of people but a builder of people who have knowledge and transform the way the academic system operates. This is neither common nor easy:

> The first time I declared the desire to work in a loving workplace, my friends acted as if I were crazy. However,

---

[6] LUIZA D', Á.; VIANA, Á.; PACIFICO DA SILVA, H. Meritocracia neoliberal e capitalismo financeiro: implicações para a proteção social e a saúde. Ciência & Saúde Coletiva, p. 2107–2117, 2017.

[7] HOOKS, bell. Ensinando comunidade: uma pedagogia da esperança. Rio de Janeiro: Elefante, 2021, p. 27. Author's translation.

[8] FREIRE, P. Educação na cidade. 2a ed. São Paulo: Cortez, 1995, p. 103. Author's translation.

> I was convinced I would work better in an environment shaped by a loving ethic[9].

Usually, when people talk about working in a loving manner, it is not taken seriously or even treated as if it were unprofessional behavior. All the discourse one usually hears about trying to work with something one likes, as they will work with it for the rest of their life, loses value in the face of professionalism and meritocratic discourse. Daring to look for another way is a challenge proposed by bell hooks, who calls us to reflect on how we want to produce scientifically and how we want to live: "[...] embracing love ethic means inserting all dimensions of love - 'care, commitment, trust, responsibility, respect and knowledge"[10].

> Commitment to a loving ethic transforms our lives by giving us different values to live by. On large and small scales, we have made choices based on the belief that honesty, frankness, and personal integrity must be expressed in public and private decisions[11].

Here lies a key to be turned because the author shows us that even in a system that structures our action towards competition and distances us from issues that affect it, the choice of commitment to loving ethics can transform the choices made and the way this is expressed in public and private spheres, both in our productive work and in the way we choose to place ourselves in spaces and in the world.

---

[9] HOOKS, bell. Tudo sobre o amor: novas perspectivas. Rio de Janeiro: Elefante, 2020, p. 86. Author's translation.

[10] Idem, p. 15.

[11] Idem, p. 105.

Methodological path

This work aims to start from a qualitative narrative research approach, from an interactionist tradition that values subjectivity, encompassing a plurality of views and conceptions about the researched object.

The choice of the focus group occurred because we sought a safe space for listening, but with interaction among the participants. The focus group was conducted using the Zoom platform, recorded and transcribed for later analysis. During the focus group, a Jamboard with anonymous participation was also made available, where participants could post insights, issues they did not wish to speak openly to the group, concerns, and other written topics about each of the questions that guided the research.

The guiding questions for the focus group were:.

- How do you feel about Administration teaching and research today?
- In what aspects can academia in the area of Administration improve?
- What actions can we take for a more loving Administration?

The analyses below were woven from the statements heard and the relationships built and established in the safe space created.

Analysis and discussion of results

The first question asked: "How do you feel about Administration teaching and research today?" We can highlight some lines that bring essential points for this chapter:

> There are lines of research, and we can agree or not. But sometimes we feel a bit constrained within academia, **with little freedom, and depending, sometimes, there is a lot of freedom**. So, it depends a lot, like on the profile and also on the relationship with the professor. I think **this relationship permeates this field of power that exists within the university**. [...] I think it has to be this plural space for debate, for dialogue, for sharing, it has to be. We must expose ourselves too, you can't be willing to accept everything (participant 5).

In this excerpt, participant 5 of the focus group mentions that the issue of freedom is essential because, in the academic environment, sometimes there is a lot of space and, other times, little freedom, leaving students uncertain about what they can or cannot do. This is complemented by the issue of the field of power that exists within the University, where those who have a lot of power end up imposing how things should be done.

> I think it's a very diverse field, but **I don't feel we talk about teaching**, I don't feel that much diversity. In teaching, I think, there are many limitations lately. This is largely due to the lack of a larger number of professors in the program. **There are few professors in the program, with few areas of knowledge. This also ends up limiting our research**. I will make a link with the research because many times we have to **align ourselves with the professors' lines of research, being unable, many times, to make our wish prevail, as researchers of things we would like to research**, out of our own free will or out of personal

interest or experience, whatever it may be. **And we end up having to go to fields that are often not so interesting** (participant 2).

Participant 2 states that little is said about teaching in the graduate program, mainly because there are few professors in the program, which limits the areas of knowledge. This means the student has to submit to the professors' lines of research, disregarding, in this case, what he really wishes to study. A sentence that draws our attention is that this situation leads students to "go to fields that are often not so interesting", taking away the shine of the research, the student's curiosity and desire to learn and research something that really makes sense to them. Related to the love ethics brought by bell hooks[12], the student within a program structure is often restricted to what can be done.

> [...] **pressure for publication** bothers me a lot. **Publishing for the sake of publishing**, things that, many times, in my opinion, do not add any value, they **only add value to the program.** [...] And so, when you look at productions about a lot of things, which are not thinking about administration, which I think is something that is very much in line with society and in line with the professional field, I don't think research is aligned with society, as a professional. **Very little research, in my opinion, ends up adding this value.** So, those are the things that bother me. Likewise, regarding teaching, I see there are less and more prepared professors [...] I think I must summarize my perceptions like this, and mine were much more / mostly negative (participant 2).

The same participant brings some discomfort, mainly in relation to the pressure for publication, a topic frequently mentioned by graduate students as well as

---

[12] HOOKS, bell. Tudo sobre o amor: novas perspectivas. Rio de Janeiro: Elefante, 2020.

academics and that is related to the meritocratic system imposed by neoliberalism, which makes everyone be evaluated by productivity[13]. The participant also highlights the issue of producing for the sake of producing, or as it is commonly said in academia, "publish or perish" (unknown author), something closely linked to the "quantitative logic of performances"[14]:

> The question is to know what "culture of results" means in justice, medicine, culture, or education, and on which values we can judge it. In fact, the act of judgment, which depends on ethical and political criteria, is replaced by an efficiency measure that is supposed to be ideologically neutral[15].

In this supposed neutrality, the ethics of the individual's production is often disregarded, as brought by participant 2. The alignment and social relevance of what is produced is also lost.

> *In this perspective, a positive thing concerning the field, the administration field, is that we have many possibilities. Having a super open field, super rich, makes one willing to do a lot of things. Really, start reading and studying. We want to do everything because everything is cool. Anyway, we can connect, we can be on. And the more complex the problems, the more multidisciplinary they are. However, this way, we need other areas to be able to solve a problem. And it is from this positive point that a little bit of how I feel comes, which is a bit of **frustration for not being able to study everything**. And maybe this has to do with the model of what academia is like. [...] **It is a very closed thing, which does not dialogue with our reality today,***

---

[13] LUIZA D', Á.; VIANA, Á.; PACIFICO DA SILVA, H. Meritocracia neoliberal e capitalismo financeiro: implicações para a proteção social e a saúde. Ciência & Saúde Coletiva, p. 2107–2117, 2017.

[14] DARDOT, P.; LAVAL, C. A nova razão do mundo: ensaio sobre a sociedade neoliberal. 1. ed. São Paulo: Boitempo, 2016, p. 313. Author's translation.

[15] Idem.

in which most students work. Most have several other tasks because they have to get by. [...] *So, in this sense, it's a little frustrating because **we want to do research. We want to go deeper** into it. I am very passionate about administration, but it seems that we cannot fit in.* ***We must adapt to the model; the model does not adapt to us.*** *This makes it more and more distant (participant 1).*

Participant 1 mentions that she feels a certain frustration for not being able to handle everything, for wishing to go deeper, but not having the time since most students are also workers and end up having limited time to dedicate to graduate studies. She also highlights academia as a very closed space that does not dialogue with students' reality. This becomes evident through students' reports about classes being scheduled in the afternoon shift, in which students commonly work, considering most students are linked to companies that usually have their working hours from 9 am to 6 pm, with small variations, forcing the student to adapt to the structure or model of the program.

Still regarding the first question, students used the Jamboard to share the following cards[16]:

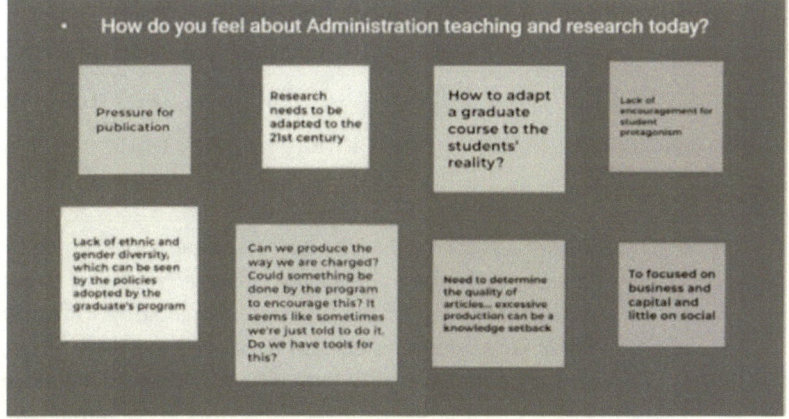

[16] Researcher's material (2022).

Some points were repeated in relation to those already highlighted in the participant's speeches, such as the pressure for publication, the need to adapt the graduate course to students' realities, and the issue of productivity, such as the need to assess the quality of the material produced by students and verify if it does not generate a setback in the production of knowledge.

In addition to these, new points emerged, such as the lack of ethnic and gender diversity, the idea that the Administration program is "too focused on business and capital and little on social" (Jamboard, unidentified interviewee), the "lack of encouragement for the protagonism of students" (Jamboard, unidentified interviewee) and the need to adapt the research carried out to the present.

The second question posed to the focus group was: "In what aspects can academia in the area of Administration improve?". Some speeches which bring important points to the reflection proposed here called our attention. The first speech was: "It's a free therapy, which you provided us with" (participant 2). This point already highlights the lack of safe listening spaces for Administration academics to express themselves. Academic life in graduate school, despite being organized in groups, becomes a lonely journey once classes are over. Another speech points out:

> We are very focused on the business area, and when we try to escape, like from the already designed model, we have a little more of difficulty. [...] **For those looking for other fields, another more critical field, we have difficulties, and it becomes a very lonely field**. It's research, but we feel alone, a little outside. [...] So, this is something **we**

> need more guidance on, and this is hardly obtained. So, I think there's a model. There is a model already within the project, and those who deviate from this model have **much more difficulty doing their research**. Consequently, they end up having to walk alone. So, they feel a little more helpless, they feel more difficulty, even the lack of a more specific class, which they try to look for in other programs (participant 5).

From this speech by participant 5, several important elements emerge for us to think about how the science of Administration can improve. It is noted that the more daring the student is, bringing the interface with other fields of knowledge, the less they fit into the hegemonic model of graduate studies, having their journey hampered by the absence of guidance, which "is hardly obtained" (participant 5). This makes one wonder how much the area, which according to its speeches seeks so much innovation, is open to working with themes beyond the knowledge its professors have expertise in, and how much this area really seeks to add new interdisciplinary or transdisciplinary knowledge to the studies produced. This is in line with the speech of participant 3, who states:

> One thing that would be important is **tools for us to get there. They want us to produce a lot of articles, you know? But what tools do we have to do this?** What kind of support do they have to do this? They have help, we don't. So, I think like this, for example, about research tools. I know they are there, in the computer lab, but they are out of date. [...] **In qualitative research, there is the difficulty in transcription.** Oh, is there any software or support for transcription to make the work faster? [...] Doing research like this? **The university wants this production**, and the works need this. I think **having tools to help students do what is proposed is important** (participant 3).

With the lack of openness to studies that challenge the already established knowledge, there is also a lack of adequate conditions for production. As highlighted above, today, the infinity of tools available to carry out research needs to be within the reach of students. It is impossible to ignore they exist and make work simpler, faster, and more enjoyable. This speech also points out there is a demand, on the part of the program and the university, for the production of articles. However, with little guidance and no adequate tools, it is much more difficult for students to fulfill what is required. As a result:

> We end up **limiting ourselves to reading many articles but going very little in-depth in theory** and theoretical discussion. Then, we are charged when it comes to preparing the work. I think that's what we have to rescue, to go a little deeper into the studies. **A deeper discussion, because I believe reading the article doesn't give you that, it doesn't give you that depth,** that this we will find in sociology. We will find this in other fields of philosophy. **Administration is taking some of this more foundational discussion out** (participant 5).

Classes end up being based, for the most part, on reading scientific articles, but even those present little theoretical depth. Paradoxically, this theoretical deepening is demanded later for the writing of projects and works, leaving students a little helpless. Another point stated is that the Administration program has little foundational discussion and works little with theories. This point is reiterated on the Jamboard.

> There are difficulties in writing and difficulties in translation. To **look at students' needs and provide extracurricular things outside**, or that you have at the

> university, or thought of by students themselves. I don't know. **It seems like we have a very rigid thing there** (participant 1).

> And they are also in the retention of people who have difficulties. I know, nowadays, **there are no quotas in this sense necessarily, but if they were created, diversity should be taken into consideration.** As I said earlier, **having things allows students to live and study. [...] Anyway, I don't believe there are retention conditions.** They are the people who have the most difficulty in terms of income, specifically, so I think that's it (participant 4).

Finally, it is mentioned the absence of affirmative action policies (quotas) in graduate studies in Administration, resulting in little diversity. Even so, the lack of conditions for the student to live and study during graduate studies, the absence of decent retention conditions within the university is highlighted.

Still regarding the second question, the students put on Jamboard the following cards[17]:

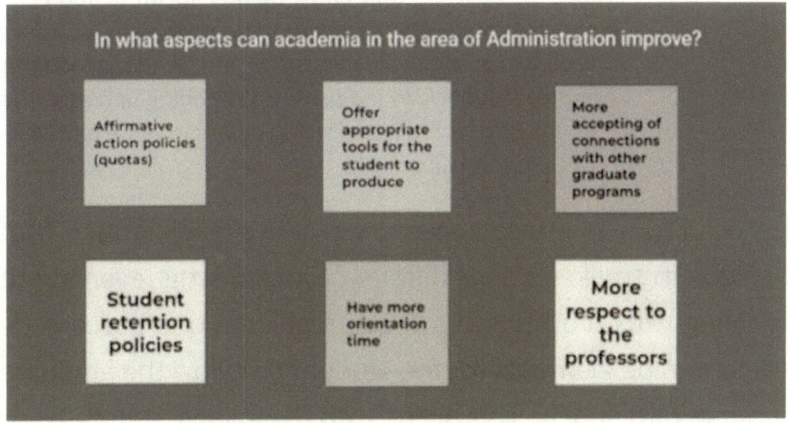

The aspects that appeared without identification refer to the points already mentioned earlier in the analysis

---
[17] Researcher's material (2022).

of students' participation in the focus group. At this point, it was just reinforcing the importance of a better opening of the Administration field to other areas, providing a wider connection with other programs, and the need for more qualified orientation time, something recurrent in the students' speeches.

The last question asked in the focus group was: "What actions can we take for a more loving Administration?". Here, in seeking change, we can highlight:

> I think we must start from within, and then I'll have to suck up / give credit to my advisor and tell you what she did at our year-end party. [...] In addition to receiving us at her home, she prepared a bag, and each one would take something out of it: an eraser, a candy, and everything had a connotation. **It was a PhD survival kit**. So, it was about writing this story of **erasing the most unpleasant moments, writing, and, in addition, the candy to sweeten it**. Something very sentimental, but so affectionate, so warm. **So, you connect with that kind of attitude and carry quality forward**. You carry forward a way of being, a way of doing things that values acceptance, that values positive and, at the same time, simple feedback, in the sense of providing opportunities for the development itself. I think that's what we must take forward (participant 3).

From this first speech, we can already notice that welcoming makes a huge difference for students, even about dealing with problems, as these small actions are already determining elements for the student to follow the graduate course with quality. This aligns with the following statement: "Balance, balance among rigor, recognition, demand, so that it comes in a more loving, more constructive way, properly speaking" (participant 2). The search for balance in graduate studies in Administration needs to go beyond individual actions and become an attitude of the program itself, which cares for everyone. One participant brings an essential element:

> Making this environment a more loving one, I think, depends on us, too. So, I'm going to bring it now to our side. So, we complain because this is missing, that is missing, the workshop is missing, the debate is missing, addressing difficulties is missing, but **we can do this. After all, we are studying for the Ph.D., or the master's, we have experience, and we can help each other** (participant 1).

Here, the participant's self-awareness brings a warning: students can also make favorable moves, such as this work, carried out in a focus group previously reported as a collective therapy session. Thus, actions can come from the students as well as from the programs, searching for a more loving Administration science. However, it is important to resume here some points already addressed before, which bring, at different times, the issue of students with few conditions to remain in the program and with little time available to think about these actions. Another important point here may be the issue of the lonely person, because when students walk alone, they end up ignoring the needs and difficulties of their colleagues. Additionally:

> **We will find in the university what we have in life**. So, these relationship issues permeate what we see within the university, and I've had moments when I felt a little welcomed and, at other times, I felt very welcomed. So, **I had a very positive experience with my colleagues**, as with all of you here. And I was helped a lot, just as I was also able to help. And **I think this exchange environment is essential for knowledge** (participant

4).

This last speech is essential, as it responds to the previous participant's comments, highlighting the role of colleagues as fundamental to the achievement of graduate work. This is very much a reflection of our society, as pointed out, because structures tend not to welcome, while people welcome each other at the most diverse occasions.

About this third question, the participating students put on Jamboard the following cards[18]:

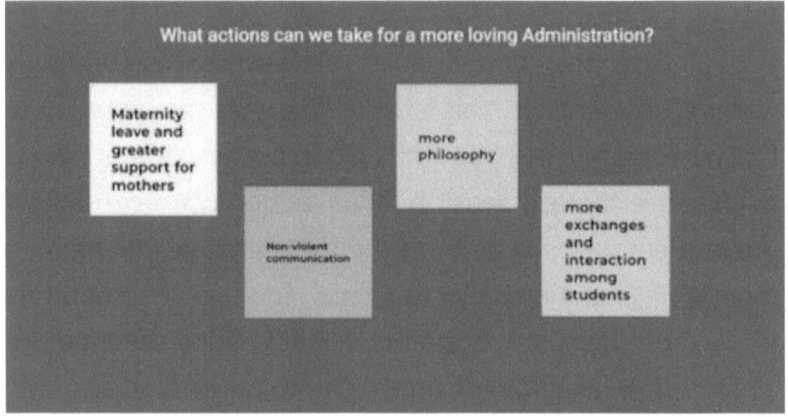

From these cards, we can highlight some delicate points that permeate the program, which did not appear in open speeches during the focus group, such as maternity leave, already recognized by the Brazilian Coordination for the Improvement of Higher Education Personnel (CAPES), but not yet implemented in the program, and the need for greater acceptance of women-mothers who attend a graduate course. The term "non-violent communication" also appeared, which indicates that communication in Administration needs to be rethought and revised towards

---
18   Researcher's material (2022).

a more loving model. Finally, in addition to the emphasis on exchanges and interactions among students, already discussed, a card with the words "more philosophy" appears, which here can be related to the aspect discussed earlier about the lack of in-depth theoretical exploration in the readings required by the program courses.

As a broad analysis of the focus group, one of the limitations found was that small initiatives can make the production of knowledge lighter and less harmful from the point of view of the individual who is occupying that space at the moment, but they cannot change the neoliberal structure that stands as the contemporary way of organizing life, that is, "a generalized commodification of social relations"[19].

To envision a more loving Administration, it is essential for science to engage a dialogue with society, so that changes may alter the current educational system, designed and aligned with the neoliberal policies introduced in Brazil from the mid-1990s onwards, which changed the structure of Brazilian Public Administration, introducing assumptions from the New Public Management[20,21,22] to the way of thinking, generating and regulating education in Brazil.

---

19   DARDOT, P.; LAVAL, C. A nova razão do mundo: ensaio sobre a sociedade neoliberal. 1. ed. São Paulo: Boitempo, 2016, p. 23. Author's translation.

20   DASSO JÚNIOR, A. É. Reforma do Estado com participação cidadã? Déficit democrático das Agências Reguladoras Brasileiras. [s.l.] Universidade Federal de Santa Catarina, 2006.

21   FAGANELLO, C. P. Balanço do gerencialismo: análise da influência do modelo de administração pública gerencial no período de 1995 a 2017 no Brasil. [s.l.] Universidade Federal do Rio Grande do Sul, 2017.

22   PAULA, A. P. P. DE. Administração pública brasileira entre o gerencialismo e a gestão social. RAE-revista de administração de empresas, v. 45, n. 1, p. 36-49, 2005.

This does not diminish all efforts to think about differentiated spaces, as proposed by bell hooks in his professional career. Being subjected to a system that makes us hostages of a capitalist mode of production, which disregards the subjectivities that challenge it, does not diminish the value of initiatives and loving ethical conduct by researchers, students, and academics in general.

The present study demonstrated that graduate students demand and need more loving spaces, exchanges, and adequate conditions to reach the end of their academic journey. Excessive demands and the lack of teaching the way / guidance are disconcerting and uncomfortable factors among the participants. In addition, this work also showed academics are aware they can take action; however, more as a possibility than as something that translates into concrete actions. This can be understood as an existing discourse that does not become a practice, mainly due to how the entire academic structure is placed and reproduced within the neoliberal logic.

Final Considerations

This text does not propose solutions, especially since the potential for academic work to generate social transformation is known. Nevertheless, it seeks to elucidate and understand, within the scope of the study, how a graduate program in Administration can contribute to a more loving science of Administration.

The analyzed reports show the need for safer listening

spaces within the academia, because from listening, the kind of listening that does not aim to judge, expose, or ignore what is being said, a process of change in the understanding of the space being occupied begins and the idea that the academic path in graduate school must be trodden alone is broken. Therefore, suffering is also something individual.

Still, this text aims to contribute in a way that some recurrent problems, such as lack of guidance, lack of support for retention, and lack of adequate research tools, can be addressed by programs that choose to reflect on the problems that affect their students.

Institutional policies also need to be revised, such as the case of greater acceptance of mothers and the provision of maternity leave. Although such policies are already regulated under the Brazilian Coordination for the Improvement of Higher Education Personnel (CAPES), the decision of their implementation, granting or not, is still at the discretion of the program. Another example is graduate affirmative action policies (quotas), highlighted by the absence of black people in the focus group members and in the analyzed program. In addition, it is essential to raise the issue of the pressure for publication, which appears as "produce for what?", which often loses its meaning for the student carrying out the research, considering that publication is taken as a mark of the success or failure of the project work, while the purpose of the study should be what it translates into real meaning.

Finally, this text presents itself as something that

intends to dislodge; based on the points raised and given, it intends to arouse interest in the production of knowledge today in Administration. However, it can also be replicated in other areas to encourage more safe listening spaces, reflection and production of knowledge that can challenge the models established and naturalized in Brazilian academia.

4

Curious Amora: looking for new forms of teaching and learning

Kelly Cebelia das Chagas do Amaral

Abstract[1]

This chapter intends to present the possibility of breaking paradigms amid restrictive traditional education systems. From early childhood to higher education, it is possible to experiment with new ways of teaching. We believe that curiosity is a primordial element in the act of learning. Very intrigued by the "lack of love" and empathy experienced in years of school teaching, this author, on a cloudy day between her ramblings, found herself surprised by the magical apparition of her inner child materialized in the art of amigurumi, which lovingly pushed her to research schools that developed different forms of teaching. For this, Amora, who, in her adult version, is a Physical Education teacher and does not give up her colored ball, equipped her backpack with courage, joy, disposition, books, theories, and discipline and went in search of schools that to work with the Waldorf pedagogical approach, as this is a worldwide network known for its characteristics. We left Jardim Florescer kindergarten school, located in the city of Londrina, Paraná, Brazil, where we talked with its manager using an attentive listening. We wanted to know about the driving elements for the institution's creation, perceptions of learning, challenges, and achievements in its trajectory since the school has only been in operation for five years. Thus, since this first researched school, Amora's eyes already had a different glow, as she perceived that changes in methodologies are possible and can generate satisfactory results with more organic, smooth, healthy, and efficient

---

[1] All photos were taken by the author.

training. In addition, during the journey, Amora realized that she was not the only one who missed love, listening, and curiosity on the school floor. All over the world, there is already a chain of teachers, philosophers, and scholars who have been preaching about the need for changes and adaptations that provide new ways of teaching and learning.

Keywords: Paradigms; Waldorf School; Curiosity

The beginning...
When Amora found curiosity...

Amora, everyone could say that it would be the name of a fruit[2], but I am sorry to say that the paradigm shift here, in this case, has already begun... Why, when reading Amora, our trained mind first takes us to the name of fruit species? Amora could also be the word *aroma*[3], if written backward, or perhaps where the letter "A" lives or the feminine of the word love. In our case, Amora has the intention of reminding us, yes, of the word love, and she will be the main character of this plot. This doll is built point by point, thread by thread, intertwined, a delicate work traced by skillful hands that dominate handcrafting art using the amigurumi technique: a manual work that requires time, metrics, patience, organization, planning... that it is about the integral formation of the human being, the results of

---

[2] Amora, in Portuguese, is the name a fruit (blackberry in English). At the same time, it is the feminine derivative of "amor", that means love in Portuguese

[3] The same word is used both in Portuguese and English, with identical meanings.

which will be fully reflected in the current social model of a country.

Amora becomes, in this text, a representative thread of this author with her curiosity, especially as a child (which is usually the phase of our lives where we ask more questions, questionings, and inquiries).

At what stage of our growth do we want to know how cars are made? How does the rain fall? What holds the moon hanging in the sky? Why this, why that? Why?

Where did our genuine curiosity go?

Where did we lose or let our curiosity fall asleep?

When did we stop being inquisitive, dreamy people, capable of transforming a simple cardboard box into an aircraft and becoming heroes to save the milky way? Who stole our dreams? Our joys? Was it the school? Or rather, the way how teaching has been replicated in most mass schools? What is the main objective of standardizing school education? What do you want to tolerate? What is the true purpose and objective of this current educational model?

These and many other doubts, anxieties, and questions made Amora doubt what was put to her in this academic environment. It was curiosity that led her to investigate and, amazingly, find hundreds of other educational teaching models. The questioning became so serious that, in the future, it will become a doctoral dissertation. On this journey of discoveries, Amora had to travel far away from her roots, all to satisfy her curiosity and desire to learn. She left the north of Brazil and went to live in the southern region, just to try to find answers to these and other questions, and it was there, in the state of Paraná, in the Araucárias frontosas city of Londrina, that she met and fell in love with a teaching model that develops its practices based on the Waldorf Pedagogy philosophy.

Understanding Waldorf Pedagogy

Rudolf Steiner, considered the creator of Anthroposophy, was a philosopher, artist, and scientist born in Croatia in 1861. He began to spread his work in Germany after being invited by a businessman in 1919, who entrusted him with the construction of a school for the children of its employees. Thus, the first school with an anthroposophical philosophy was founded, based on 7-year observation and human development[4] phases[5].

Waldorf pedagogy arrived in Brazil around 1956, in the city of São Paulo, by Rudolf Lanz. For him, the school should be at the service of the child and not vice versa. The educational system should be shaped in such a way that any human being, up to the age of 18, can learn and receive an education that aims at the full development of their personality, and not at professional preparation[6].

The following are characteristics of Waldorf schools:

Wooden physical spaces; plenty of green space; emphasis on work and artistic activities; low number of students per class; teacher autonomy; active participation of families; differentiated evaluation, not using textbooks; emphasis on current and practical subjects; extracurricular activities, such as excursions and trips; and the use of eurythmy, which according to Mioto[7] is the

> Expression through body movements, which was invented by Rudolf Steiner in partnership with his wife Maria Steiner, in 1912. It is a unique art of

---

[4] FARIA, Fernanda Luiza; REIS, Ivoni Freitas. Um Estudo Sobre Escolas com Pedagogias Diferenciadas: A Pedagogia Waldorf, A Pedagogia Montessori e a Escola Da Ponte em Foco. Revista Interfaces da Educação, Paranaíba, v. 8, n. 23, p. 160-181, 2017.

[5] The "seven years" are each period of 7 years of life, which for anthroposophy represent essential cycles of development and learning.

[6] LANZ, Rudolf. A pedagogia Waldorf: caminho para um ensino mais humano. 6. ed. São Paulo: Antroposófica, 1998, p. 105.

[7] MIOTO, Luis Henrique. Escolas não-convencionais: Um estudo sobre dispositivos pedagógicos inovadores. Tese (Doutorado em Educação) – Departamento de Educação – Universidade Estadual de Londrina, Londrina, 2020, p. 425.

Anthroposophy, which has its foundations in this spiritual science. It is understood as a form of language that uses music and movement to express itself and also to balance the internal forces of the physical, etheric, soulful bodies and the body of the Self. It is part of the curriculum in Waldorf schools; the words of poetry are danced.

Entering Jardim Alvorecer Waldorf Pedagogy School in Londrina

And the day arrives for Amora to see the long-awaited school in person: her little hair was all bristling with curiosity. The path to the place is already charming, with a red clay street, few houses, and many trees. Upon entering, the appearance of a house immediately jumped out at her, and then we came across a large space with trees, a vegetable garden under construction, a playground made of wood, and what was most difficult for Amora to control: a large playpen of sand. Oh! what a desire to get rid of the researcher and run to the sand, sit down, and build great castles!

However, one of those responsible for the school was already waiting for us and told us a little about its history. Curious as she is, Amora sat down and devoted herself to listening attentively to that testimony.

Jardim Alvorecer is an Early Childhood Education Center based on Waldorf Pedagogy. It welcomes children from 2 to 6 years old and provides a different school experience from the traditional one.

The space is permeated by art, and healthy food, and nature abounds. The school started its activities in February 2017 and has the capacity to receive up to 40 children.

According to the interviewed manager, the initiative to create a new school was mainly due to the affinity and approach to anthroposophical studies, combined with the interest of four teachers (and mothers) who were part of a group and idealized that their children could experience and study with pedagogical experiences of this teaching model. Although there are more than 100 Waldorf schools spread throughout Brazil, its arrival in the city of Londrina was only possible due to this restlessness and movement of the group of mothers.

Incidentally, this has been a common element seen in other teaching models that seek pedagogical alternatives different from those found in "conventional" schools: restlessness and dissatisfaction are motivating factors for the search for new possibilities in school dynamics; the protagonists of the process are the mobilizers of change. An example of this dynamic is the so-called Learning Communities, which aim to transform the relations of their cultural, school, and social environments in their own territory, always having dialogue as their main tool. The diversity of subjects and their knowledge are validated and recognized[8].

One of the characteristics of Waldorf schools is its collective, shared management: this is what happens in Jardim Alvorecer, where dialogue is present in decision-making, which happens through meetings and assemblies. And the management of teachers has no hierarchy: everyone has the autonomy to lead their class with children and families. There is a collegiate body, but it is horizontal, there is no hierarchy.

In view of what was exposed by the interviewee, we realize that this school develops a pedagogical proposal towards differentiated teaching that involves aspects from the physical and structural environment, as well as human

---

[8] VICENTIM, Fabiana Moreira. Comunidade de Aprendizagem: Novas Práticas em Educação. Brasília: UnB, 2018.

training, both for teachers and students, insofar as[9]:

> *seeks to stimulate thinking, feeling and wanting in a balanced way, so that he, as an adult, can be what he came to be, a free person... We try to see the individual and not just the collective (Interviewed Manager).*

At the time of this speech, Amora was thoughtful... she was intrigued by the freedom and dialogue presented. Her childhood memories came to mind, memories that mark a primordial student phase of human development. She seemed to hear the teacher's voice asking to get in line, always from the smallest to the largest, and since she was tall, she already knew that she would always be the last to arrive in the classrooms to pick up the lunch or to hand over the notebook. She remembered the lack of freedom of being able to say how she felt, what she liked, and even the possibility of choosing where to sit: if autonomy and freedom cannot be developed in the school environment, where can we learn it? Paulo Freire states that "education, as a practice of freedom, is an act of knowledge, a critical approach to reality"[10].

Amora, here, as she is just our childhood guideline, knows that the past cannot be changed. However, her adult and teaching version is happy to be able to make different methodological choices, which can provide an organic development for each child.

---

[9] To work as a teacher in Waldorf schools it is necessary to take specific courses, linked to the anthroposophical philosophy, and offered by the institution

[10] FREIRE, Paulo. Conscientização: teoria e prática da libertação: uma introdução ao pensamento de Paulo Freire. Tradução de Kátia de Mello e Silva; revisão técnica de Benedito Eliseu Leite Cintra. São Paulo: Cortez & Moraes, 1979, p. 15. Disponível em: https://www.fpce.up.pt/ciie/sites/default/files/Paulo%20Freire%20-%20Conscientiza%C3%A7%C3%A3o_pp.5-19.pdf Acesso em: 11 out. 2022.

Conclusion

Amora left the visit delighted with what she witnessed in this learning space. The airy environment, full of nature, conveyed coziness - as it is a school that structurally maintains the characteristics of a wooden house - seemed welcoming, giving the impression of having less impact on the strangeness that is so peculiar to children in their first days of school. Something remarkable were also the perceptions during the interviewee's narrative: dedication, love, affection, and respect for the child's world were perceived and, therefore, the importance of offering them an education that values and considers their stages of growth and human needs.

We know that educational issues in Brazil still have a long way ahead, and we are the result of a historical process of colonization. Prioritizing Education and rethinking the oppressive and castrating form of some of its teaching methods becomes increasingly urgent. These may once have been significant but should be questioned today, given all the evolution experienced by humankind. May Amora's curiosity be present in each of us, teachers and opinion makers, making us question whether our pedagogical approaches are aligned with a quality education that is more loving and truly effective in the integral formation of human beings. Being able to step on the floor of this Waldorf school and experience its pedagogical practices made us want to get to know other existing pedagogical initiatives up close, including in some public schools. This should be the case of the Learning Community in the city of Paranoá, Brasília, Brazil, and Campos Sales school, in the community of Heliópolis, in greater São Paulo, some examples of institutions that dared to do things differently: they did not bow down to a rigid curriculum and adapted their pedagogical practices to a teaching that makes sense to their students. After all, true education is for LIFE.

5

Memories and pandemic diasporas:
learnings and a short film

Paulo de Tarso Xavier Sousa Junior

Abstract

This chapter immerses itself in the subjective affects caused by the Covid-19 scenario as the driving curiosity that delimited this writing. Curiosity is evoked based on how the pandemic lived in Brazil since 2020 contributed to shaping relationships, ways of life, and (un)built perceptions. Our objective is to understand how people hoped in the face of the consequences promoted by the Sars-CoV-2 virus through the production of a short film. Residents of Teresina, Piauí, Brazil, of different genders and ages, were heard by means of an open conversation delimited by two questions: how do you see the Covid-19 pandemic? and how do you expect the future to be in a post-pandemic Brazilian scenario? Based on this listening, it was possible to observe changes in individual and interpersonal behavior, requiring greater collective and mutual support. Facing losses and consequences, the voices report on the need to hope for the here and now, in the face of the wounds and scars felt by the population due to the Brazilian federal government's inertia in the fight against the virus. Only then will it be possible to materialize a society with greater empathy, equity, and above all, love between beings.

Keywords: Transformations; Self-care; Hope.

Introduction

> "I learned that courage is not the absence of fear, but the triumph over it"
>
> Nelson Mandela

Thinking about the Covid-19 pandemic may seem, currently, in the middle of 2023, a little distant for many people. However, this period became longer than expected and/or imagined. Until then, societies knew very little or almost nothing about the health consequences of this virus. In addition, this pathology also presented a series of significant changes in societies and in everyday structures. Almeida et al.[1] point out that several changes in the forms of survival and human relationships could be observed in Brazil. These transformations presented even more difficulties in terms of health, income, and life maintenance conditions.

Malta et al.[2] warn about how Brazilian men and women dealt with so many setbacks arising amidst the pandemic. Many risk behaviors linked to poor health conditions were observed, putting these individuals face to face with their finitude. This represented the presence of more illnesses in the population in the face of this state of health emergency, resulting in more situations of vulnerability and suffering.

---

[1] ALMEIDA, Wanessa da Silva de et al. Mudanças nas condições socioeconômicas e de saúde dos brasileiros durante a pandemia de COVID-19. Revista Brasileira de Epidemiologia, v. 23, 2020.

[2] MALTA, Deborah Carvalho et al. A pandemia da COVID-19 e as mudanças no estilo de vida dos brasileiros adultos: um estudo transversal, 2020. Epidemiologia e Serviços de Saúde, v. 29, n. 4, p. e2020407, 2020.

Perceptions regarding the pandemic were built based on the conditions each subject had to face. Thinking about Brazil, a country with continental dimensions and multiple realities, the virus provoked more challenges to everyday life, causing distinctions between each person's affects. Despite the widespread sharing of the phrase "we are on the same boat" on social and everyday networks, the reality was not really like this.

The great transformations experienced in this period emerged not only from the need to take care of oneself in the face of the virus contagion, but also because of security measures and how to maintain other aspects of daily life such as housing, education, work, and income. Various aspects of human life significantly changed, as well as territories, leading to reconfigurations in the face of the new reality[3].

Meanwhile, the pandemic continued to spread various vulnerabilities and social inequalities. It would be unfair to attribute the consequences of daily life changes to this health context alone since these contrasts were already plaguing the world and stemmed from a colonial heritage, which is still sustained. On the other hand, the pandemic has enhanced the wealth of so many elitist

---

[3] MEDEIROS Ana Paula; RAJS, Soraya. AS CIDADES E A PANDEMIA: EFEITOS, DESAFIOS E TRANSFORMAÇÕES. In: MENDES, Amanda; VINAGRE, Ana Beatriz; AMORIM, Annibal; CHAVEIRO, Eguimar; MACHADO, Machado; VASCONCELLOS, Luiz Carlos Fadel; GERTNER, Sonia. Diálogos sobre acessibilidade, inclusão e distanciamento social: TERRITÓRIOS EXISTENCIAIS NA PANDEMIA. – IdeiaSUS/Fiocruz; Comitê Fiocruz pela Acessibilidade e Inclusão de Pessoas com Deficiência; Departamento de Direitos Humanos, Saúde e Diversidade Cultural da Escola Nacional de Saúde Pública Sergio Arouca (DIHS/Ensp/Fiocruz); e Universidade Federal de Goiás (UFG). 6-9, 2020.

groups, causing a true abyss that separates many[4].

Amid so many adversities, an alternative came with the sharing of a concept developed by Paulo Freire (1921-1997) called "to hope" Here, the author distinguishes it from the etymology of the noun hope, bringing a new meaning to its practice.

> I do not want to say, however, that because I am hopeful, I attribute to my hope the power to transform reality and, thus convinced, I start the fight without taking into account the concrete, material data, affirming that my hope is enough. My hope is necessary but not enough. She alone does not win the fight, but without it, the fight weakens and falters. We need critical hope, like fish need clean water[5].

In this way, hoping consists of an action, not based only on a desire but on seeking a mobilization in the here and now. In a chaotic scenario full of adversity caused by Covid-19, how did people manage to keep hoping? This question portrays the curiosity that kicked off the entire construction narrated in this text.

The present chapter has the general objective of understanding how people hoped in the face of the consequences promoted by the arrival of the Sars-CoV-2 virus, through the production of a short film. In addition to contributing as one more scientific production that strengthens science, the short film represents a tangible metamorphosis that actually reaches people, thus

---

[4] COSTA, António Firmino da. DESIGUALDADES SOCIAIS E PANDEMIA. In: CARMO, Renato Miguel do; TAVARES, Inês; CÂNDIDO, Ana Filipa (orgs.) Um Olhar Sociológico sobre a Crise Covid-19 – Lisboa, Observatório das Desigualdades, CIES-Iscte, 2020.

[5] FREIRE, Paulo. Pedagogia da Esperança: um reencontro com a Pedagogia do Oprimido. 24ª ed. São Paulo/Rio de Janeiro: Paz e Terra, 2018, p. 9.

popularizing academic and popular knowledge.

Light, camera... action!

The construction of this product (the short film) came from completing a special course in the Graduate program at a Brazilian public federal university. The activity consisted of producing a work that expressed a curiosity applied to a form of listening and that represented some aspect of lovingness in its genesis. The doubt came from the objective outlined in this work, choosing the modality of an audiovisual production as a way to carry out full listening without any kind of interference from the author of this writing.

Five people of different ages of human development and of different genders were chosen, despite the greater predominance of females. Respondents should answer two questions from the interviewer, respectively: how do you see the Covid-19 pandemic? And what do you expect the future to look like in a post-pandemic scenario?

The responses had an average duration of approximately one and a half minutes, and everyone could freely speak. Still, on the occasion, a free drawing was made with the children who participated in the production, which also expressed the views of the interviewees. After collecting these perceptions, the video was built and edited using the responses. After the completion of the short film, this chapter focuses on the questions that emerged from the memories and many diasporas experienced.

Scene one, take one

The first point concerns how the pandemic was managed by the bodies of the Brazilian federal government elected in 2018. The difficulties reflected in people's daily lives and even experienced by each of the participants of this work were made possible due to the neglect of public authorities in handling the fight against the virus. This meant taking responsibility for the countless losses, not only physical, found in this country. Marques and Raimundo[6] (2021) discuss how hate speech, fueled by representatives of these governmental spheres, produced discredit in the face of the virus itself, as well as science.

When applied to another reality, present in the children participating in this work, the pandemic represented a difficult moment since it separated them from the world and the actions they were used to, which produced some kind of well-being. Despite the technological alternatives to the loss of physical contact, experiential exchanges became quite difficult. It is possible to observe how the virus presented weaknesses to people's comfort. When invited to represent these phenomena in the form of a drawing, we can find below some examples:

---

[6] MARQUES, Ronualdo; RAIMUNDO, Jerry Adriano. O Negacionismo científico refletido na pandemia da covid-19. Boletim de Conjuntura (BOCA), v. 7, n. 20, p. 67-78, 2021.

 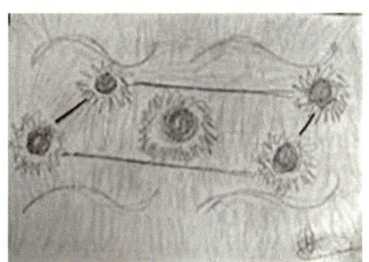

Source: Author (2023)

The virus is conceived as a great villain, and negative representations are attributed to it. These visions come from the consequences provoked - and not experienced before - by a large part of the population, since phenomena such as the pandemic did not occur for many centuries.

Based on the drawings produced before the short film, emojis related to emotions and feelings such as anger and sadness were attributed to Covid-19, demonstrating how the pandemic caused several mishaps, directly reflecting on people's mental health.

Garrido and Rodrigues[7] discuss the impact of Covid-19 beyond social changes and human health: its effects presented fears to the population in the face of finitude and impacted various social sectors. The pandemic put people in front of adverse scenarios and a lack of

---

[7] GARRIDO, Rodrigo Grazinoli; RODRIGUES, Rafael Coelho. Restrição de contato social e saúde mental na pandemia: possíveis impactos das condicionantes sociais. Journal of health & biological sciences, v. 8, n. 1, p. 1-9, 2020.

planning for future possibilities, thus having a great impact on their subjectivities. It is not by chance that there is emotional distress associated with this entire period.

The pandemic still represented, as observed in the recordings, changes in how people led their lives. New behaviors were adopted to build protection against the virus, but some issues and dilemmas were brought up as reflections: would other people have access to these tools? Indeed, not everyone was in the same boat.

The discussions also showed uncertainties regarding Brazil. Faced with the fatalities imposed by the virus, the country was still facing a serious crisis in many aspects: more than 37 million people were infected and more than 600,000 died from Covid-19[8]. Uncertainties produced anxieties, as well as fear of the virus and the future. How dreams and plans would be built? And those who had one and/or several losses, how would they move forward? These are questions that still remain unanswered.

The pandemic developed a major crisis in various social aspects; however, Brazil was still subjected to many other ills. The impressive death toll goes beyond the negligence of the public authorities. It also reflects the face of denialism and the many actions carried out daily that enhance the virus. In this sense, the losses were blamed for so many other situations that it becomes hard to think

---

[8] BRASIL. Ministério da Saúde. DATASUS – Departamento de Informática do SUS. Secretaria de Vigilância em Saúde. Coronavírus / Brasil. Covid-19 Painel Coronavírus. Brasília: DF, 2023.

about how everything could be experienced differently[9].

Scene two, take one

> Without minimum hope, we cannot even begin the fight, but without the fight, hope, as an ontological necessity, is lost, unaddressed and becomes hopelessness that, at times, extends into tragic despair. Hence the need for a certain education in hope. It has such importance in our existence, individual and social, that we must not experience it in the wrong way, letting it slip into hopelessness and despair. Hopelessness and despair, consequence and raison d'etre of inaction or immobility[10].

In this scene, the discussions are based on how each one sees or sees a way out, a possibility or hope, even with the extreme threats presented by Covid-19. An example was the countless "diasporas" experienced, which separated and distanced people, situations, and contexts. Based on these abrupt changes, each one sought, in their own way and within their own context, to develop resilient strategies towards a more effective change related to the difficulties imposed on their daily lives.

The Brazilian 2022 presidential elections represented hope for the participants. According to Ferrari[11] the choice of representatives by the Brazilian population did not leave out the debate of the problems experienced during the pandemic. A lot of disinformation was used to maintain a

---

9 PEREIRA, Carlos; MEDEIROS, Amanda; BERTHOLINI, Frederico. O medo da morte flexibiliza perdas e aproxima polos: consequências políticas da pandemia da COVID-19 no Brasil. Revista de Administração Pública, v. 54, p. 952-968, 2020.

10 FREIRE, Paulo. Pedagogia da Esperança: um reencontro com a Pedagogia do Oprimido. 24. ed. São Paulo/Rio de Janeiro: Paz e Terra, 2018, p. 11.

11 FERRARI, Carlos Kusano Bucalen. IMPACTO DAS ELEIÇÕES NA REEMERGÊNCIA DE COVID-19 NO BRASIL. Boletim de Conjuntura (BOCA), v. 8, n. 22, p. 151-160, 2021.

government that had not acted in favor of the population during the fight against the virus.

Change through voting comes as a practical and active form of hope, focusing mainly on youth as protagonists in changing the country. Thus, the short film reflects on the transformations that come from this exercise of collective citizenship and how it influences a society torn apart in many ways by a pandemic.

Religion represented a point of warmth, strength, and resilience during Covid-19 to the participants of this work. Andrade et al.[12] discuss the importance of these beliefs in the face of a dystopian situation full of ills. Religion, regardless of what it is, has this ability to help and is often considered to be largely responsible for day-to-day support.

The reflections continued about how to return to a "normal" life. At first this term is questioned, since after so many changes, how to move forward? There were losses and non-beneficial transformations in many spaces and for many realities. At that moment, the term "new normal" appears pointing to a new way of moving forward, reframing (or not) the ills, readapting reality and aiming for alternatives to continue surviving.

Aguiar and Araújo[13] discuss what this new beginning would be like. The pandemic concreteness cannot be seen

---

[12] ANDRADE, Ivani Coelho et al. O fenômeno religioso na pandemia da COVID-19. Último Andar, v. 24, n. 38, p. 113-125, 2021.

[13] AGUIAR, Raquel; ARAÚJO, Inesita Soares de. A Fábula do viroceno: As narrativas sobre heroísmo, solidariedade e novo normal. Revista Latinoamericana de Ciencias de la Comunicación, v. 19, n. 35, 2020.

as a fairy tale that will have a happy ending plus a moral. Understanding the pandemic scenario in this way points to the erasure of millions of stories that were torn apart and memories that did not have a happy ending. On the contrary, people are still trying to rebuild themselves and get rid of so many adversities in a row.

Chico Buarque would say: "in spite of you, tomorrow will be another day"[14]. This was one of the mottos observed in this initiative. Although the participants did not believe that society would be the same, they hoped to allow people to seek and mobilize forces so that they could face up to the stricken problems, reiterating their rights and the duties of the State. This point should not be seen as a revengeful telenovela plot. On the contrary, these pains result in the resumption of the direction of the short film of each of their lives, because "you will pay and it will be doubled, every tear shed in my pain"[15].

Final sequence

Without a doubt, the Covid-19 pandemic changed the world and left pain in people's memories (those who managed to survive it), suffering and so many other emotions and feelings that would be impossible to describe in these lines. Listening to what these people have to say and how they saw this period of turmoil is part of the genesis of this work.

---

[14] BUARQUE, Chico; MPB4; QUARTETO EM CY. Apesar de você. Universal Music Ltda: 1978.
[15] Idem.

The hope outlined here and so well portrayed by Paulo Freire returns to the everyday scenario in an unexpected and necessary way. Although many do not conceive its meaning in written form, it is found in their actions and even in their speeches. It is now up to each one of you, not only the participants of this product but also you, readers, to continue being part of this great collective of struggles. Count on you!

Cut!

Note of the author: The short film reported in this chapter is not available on digital platforms due to sound/image rights of the people involved.

6

Dialogues with teachers:
technology and continuing teacher education

Ana Paula André

Abstract

This chapter is based on the proposal to listen to teachers in continuing education on digital technologies through curiosity about the subject and from the perspective of active listening to the other. Historically, Digital Information and Communication Technologies in the school context (DICT) and their daily use in education have always been permeated by resistance in teaching activities and by few public policies and investments. Such factors lead, therefore, to the lack of training of educators regarding its use. In this sense, in this research, sixteen teachers who work in the State Public Network in the city of Cascavel, Paraná, Brazil, were heard through semi-structured questionnaires. The need to investigate the theme emerges in a troubled historical moment, in which it is necessary to rethink the implications of technologies in the school context, demanding greater depth, readings, dialogues, and understanding of what is required to prepare critical students. This invites us to reflect on teacher education processes. The research made it possible to understand what teachers consider as continuing education in technology and how it could contribute to their practice.

Keywords: Listening, Teacher education, Technology

Introduction

Through the course **Listening, Curiosity, and Love** of the Graduate Program in History of Sciences and Techniques and Epistemology at the Federal University of Rio de Janeiro (UFRJ), we sought a research object that would materialize the research need and that could be the path to what we wanted to know. This search was permeated by the dialogical nature of lovingly listening to others and carrying out permanent sharing within the construction of knowledge, based on the understanding that "learning is not passively absorbing something already ready, outside of us, but interacting with what is learned to transform our way of thinking and acting"[1].

The innovative character of **Listening, Curiosity, and Love** differed from traditional graduate courses format, allowing the collective construction with all those involved, favoring the conscious choice of bibliographic references, exchanges, sharing, and even the dynamics used in class.

Thus, the search for understanding of what, at first, was unknown to us permeated "curiosity as an inquiring restlessness, as an inclination to reveal something, as a question verbalized or not, as a search for clarification, as a sign of attention that suggests alertness, is an integral part of the vital phenomenon, [...] critical, dissatisfied, restless curiosity"[2].

---

[1] Mariotti, 2000, cited by Pires, L. L. de A. et al. A Educação de Jovens e adultos: o educando e o contexto da pandemia. Itinerarius Reflectionis, 16(1), 2020, p. 13. Available at: https://doi.org/10.5216/rir.v16i1.65616. Acessed on: 21.02.2022. Free translation.

[2] Freire, P. Pedagogia da Autonomia: Saberes necessários à prática educativa. Paz e Terra: Rio de Janeiro, 2021, p. 33. Free translation.

With such concern, we started with the question of what to research, followed by how to explore a approach that represented the dialogical character, active listening, and interaction with the construction of this proposal. With that, having defined what to research and, more explicitly, what moved me towards this need as a researcher, the aspects for carrying out the investigation were delimited.

Emphatically, what brought me to the need for research was intrinsically linked to the continuing teacher education of elementary and high school professionals about educational technologies. Since "belonging to the technological world does not mean just an adaptive limit, but requires the appropriation of pedagogies that demystify and lead to a critical look"[3]. In addition, there is also the fact that continuing education is based on

> [...] a successive process of professional development of teacher educators in the face of an interconnection between their initial graduation, corresponding to their learning experience in educational institutions, and the continuing one, which is configured as a process during the exercise of the profession.[4]

Thus, it is assumed that there is an urgent need to dialogue with such questions based on readings and discussions that allow a more dynamic approach centered on educator training and the conscious and reflective use of DICT in the school context.

---

[3] Habowski, A.; Conte, E. (Re)pensar as tecnologias na educação a partir da teoria crítica. São Paulo: Pimenta Cultural, 2019, p. 34. Free translation.

[4] Medeiros, L. M. B.; Bezerra, C. C. Algumas considerações sobre a formação continuada de professores a partir das necessidades formativas em novas tecnologias na educação. In: Sousa, R. P., et al. (Eds.) Teorias e práticas em tecnologias educacionais [online]. Campina Grande: EDUEPB, 2016, pp. 17-37, p. 23. Free translation.

Methodology

Reading and analyzing a theoretical framework on the subject made it possible to broaden the look at the theme. Using a semi-structured questionnaire, dialogue was promoted with teachers from the State Public Network in the city of Cascavel, in the countryside of Paraná, Brazil, who worked at Elementary II and High Schools.

At first, a series of questions was elaborated. It allowed us to know the educator, their time in the profession, and how they understood the use of technologies in the classroom in post-pandemic contexts: "in the permanent education of teachers, the fundamental moment is critical reflection on practice. It is by thinking critically about today's or yesterday's practice that the next practice can be improved"[5].

The survey was applied to sixteen professionals using Google Forms. Only one of the interviewees chose not to answer all the proposed questions. He also did not answer the open questions.

The professionals who participated in the research work in the same network as the researcher (State Public Network), and, to complement their income, they also work in private and Municipal schools at different educational levels. The subjects taught by the research participants were Portuguese, Art, Mathematics, History, Geography, Physical Education, English, Religion, and Science. The highest

---

[5] Freire, P. Pedagogia da autonomia: saberes necessários à prática educativa. São Paulo: Paz e Terra, 2011, p. 60. Free translation.

percentage of professors per subject occurred in Art and Geography (20% each).

Results and discussion

The use of technologies within classrooms in on the rise, even as methodologies. However, not always with a conscious and reflective approach. Educating in a world guided by this use of technologies implies transiting through new Brito and Ferreira[6] and "exploring the languages of digital media and their ways of interpreting and constructing reality." In this sense,

> [...] learning and teaching in the digital environment involves the construction of a critical, responsible and solidary action to ensure qualified access to technology as equal opportunities and possibilities in the face of all the diversity of challenges posed by the digital culture.[7]

In this perspective, with Google Forms, interaction with teachers began by carrying out an initial mapping, in which it was possible to obtain the following answers about the time of teaching activity:

---

[6] Brito, G. S.; Ferreira, J. L. Tecnologias na educação presencial e a distância em tempos de cibercultura: a formação do professor. In: Brito, G. S. (Ed.). Cultura, escola e processos formativos em educação: percursos metodológicos e significativos. Rio de Janeiro: BG Business Graphics Editora, 2020, p. 78. Available at: <https://businessgraphics.com.br/wp-content/uploads/2020/12/CULTURAESCOLA-E-PROCESSOS-FORMATIVOS-EM-EDUCACAO.pdf> Acessed on: 30 mar. 2023. Free translation.

[7] Fantin, M.; Rivotella, P. C. Crianças na era digital: desafios da comunicação e da educação. REU, Sorocaba, SP, v. 36, n. 1, p. 89-104, jun. 2010, p. 11-12. Available at: https://educacao-digital35.webnode.com/_files/200000005-0c6d30e603/01_Fantin_2006.pdf. Acessed on: 10 jan. 2023. Free translation.

Image 1 - Time working as a teacher

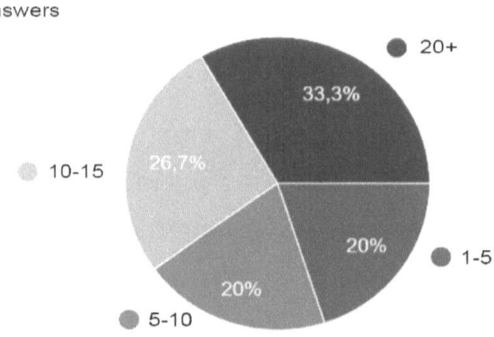

Source: Researcher's material (2022).

This aspect allowed us to observe that most teachers who participated in the research (33.3%) had been working for twenty or more years.

Following this question, we asked about the subjects they teach, as represented in the figure below, which highlights a transdisciplinary need for education-focused technology.

Image 2 - Subjects taught

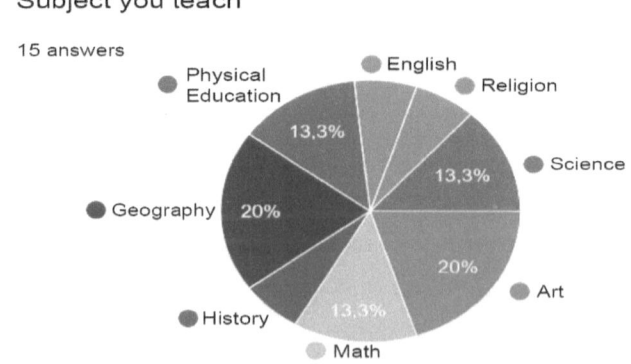

Source: Researcher's material (2022).

In addition to these issues, questions about the immersion of teachers in the use of educational technologies during the pandemic were emphasized. On this issue, a very representative number of professionals (62.5%) considered the training unsatisfactory and superficial.

It was possible to perceive that the continuing education for the use of educational technologies by public school teachers, in addition to being fragmented in the pandemic period, had other serious obstacles, among which the costs of equipment or training, assumed by the teachers themselves to work from home. Once again, we could notice the materialization of the minimum state policy, leaving the educators with the burden of the expenses needed to develop their work.

Image 3 - Teachers' immersion in the use of educational technologies during the pandemic

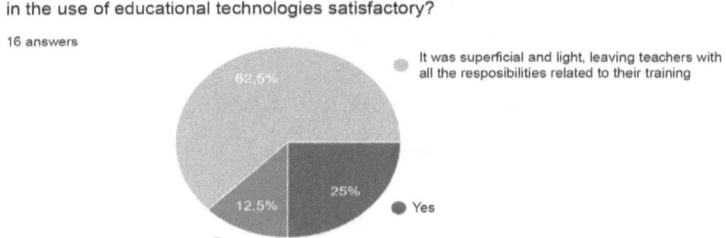

Source: Researcher's material (2022).

The following question showed a high percentage of positive responses from teachers regarding that educational technologies can help in-person teaching and learning, enabling students to participate more effectively (66.7% agree with this aspect, as seen in the table below).

Image 4 - Educational technologies as allies in the learning process

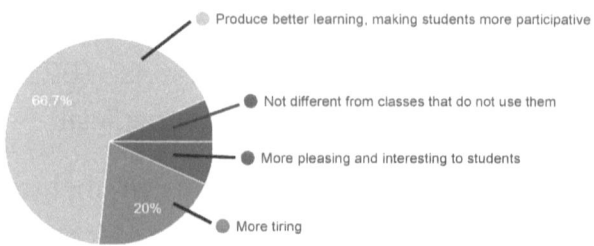

Source: Researcher's material (2022).

An open-ended questionnaire was also applied to the participants, in which they could express their understanding of the theme. The questionnaire addressed the following questions:

1. With today's real educational conditions, how do you work with technology in the classroom?

2. How would you like to work?

3. How can we work with the use of technologies in an emancipatory way?

4. Regarding technology, what do you consider essential in teachers' work?

It is important to highlight some statements of the teachers who participated in the research to better understand the reality of each one and their understanding and use of technologies. Asked about how he would like to work using technologies as pedagogical tools, interviewee "A" cited the lack of investments for the democratization of such resources: "I would like to be able to use technological resources in all schools I work. However, I understand that social needs do not allow the democratization of technological resources" (participant A).

According to the sharing and exchange between the teachers, continuing teacher education is usually superficial. Investments in the sector appear to be small compared to the needs presented by educational institutions:

> *This is the "x" of the question. I believe that, first, there must be training for teachers to use these new resources and adapt to the reality of the institution they work for. Many problematizations and experiments must be done to combine technology with education (participant A).*

It was also emphasized that continuing education is not characterized as a dialogical space - between speaking and listening - as it does not allow for new possibilities to be reflected in the classroom and, more explicitly, in student learning. Continuing education increasingly focus on instrumental aspects of technologies, however, it is necessary to go further to favor the possibility for teachers, through technologies, to redo readings, to question who they are and what their instruments are for, taking this into their educational practice and enhancing critical views. Therefore, "continuing learning is essential in our profession [...] it should focus on two pillars: the teacher himself, as an agent, and the school, as a place of permanent professional growth"[8].

> *Technologies are means by which the teacher can develop significant pedagogical practices that contribute qualitatively to the teaching and learning process, aiming*

---

[8] Nóvoa, 2001, cited by Freitas, S. L; Pacífico, J. M. Formação continuada: um estudo colaborativo com professores do Ensino Médio de Rondônia. Interações: Campo Grande, MS, v. 21, n. 1, p. 141-153, jan./mar. 2020, p. 144. Free translation.

at a humanizing and non-alienating education. However, it is necessary to reflect on this and which technological resources are suitable for teaching (Participant B).

From participant "B" we understood that we need to go beyond what the precise limits show us, that is, to reflect on the processes and uses of technologies within the school and in practices involving communities. In the understanding of Corradini and Misukami[9], when we consider technology only as a means of leisure or quick information, we fail to enhance their educational character and only perpetuate ideologies.

Exchanges and sharing, with their transdisciplinary character, help this dialogical and reflective process, as demonstrated by the answers to question four: what do you consider essential on the role of teachers about technologies? Ten of the fifteen participants highlighted participation in study groups and workshops that problematize the subject; one showed initial training in the area; and four highlighted the permanent exchanges with other professionals and professors to contemplate different subjects.

Technology itself, without critical reading and thinking, may only inform. It needs adequate treatment by educators so that it can qualitatively compose the teaching-learning process. Decoding and using platforms are far below what we need inside schools.

---

[9] Corradini, S. N.; Misukami, M. G. N. Práticas pedagógicas e o uso da informática. Revista Exitus, v. 3, n. 2, jul./dez., 2013, p. 85-92. Available at: <http://ufopa.edu.br/portaldeperiodicos/index.php/revistaexitus/article/view/152> Acessed on: 30 mar. 2023. Free translation.

> Students in schools today [...], due to the 2020 pandemic, are experiencing this new reality that has not yet been thought of and not projected. Therefore, the teacher must have his eyes on the present but with a look to the future, pushing students towards this reality that presents itself or will present itself in educational institutions. From this observation, it is essential that, together with the specific knowledge of education that any teacher should have when exercising their profession, technological competence is developed[10].

According to Sá et al.[11], we are clear about the State's obligations in financing and investing in public education. Structural digital resources and those that encourage continuing teacher education provide media literacy and to favor new readings for critical awareness.

It is a great challenge to reflexively understand the role and functions of technology in the educational praxis, but it may provide educators with new possibilities for interaction.

Final considerations

Given the theoretical basis and the carried-out research, issues related to the pandemic process of COVID-19 emerged and deepened new needs and other

---

[10] Brito, G. S.; Ferreira, J. L. Tecnologias na educação presencial e a distância em tempos de cibercultura: a formação do professor. In: Brito, G. S. (Ed.). Cultura, escola e processos formativos em educação: percursos metodológicos e significativos. Rio de Janeiro: BG Business Graphics Editora, 2020, p. 78. Available at: <https://businessgraphics.com.br/wp-content/uploads/2020/12/CULTURAESCOLA-E-PROCESSOS-FORMATIVOS-EM-EDUCACAO.pdf> Acessed on: 30 mar. 2023. Free translation.

[11] Sá, R. A; Luiz, L. S.; Santos, T. W. Investigação complexa sobre os processos de formação e integração das tecnologias e mídias digitais na educação. In: Brito, G. S. (Ed.). Cultura, escola e processos formativos em educação: percursos metodológicos e significativos. Rio de Janeiro: BG Business Graphics Editora, 2020. Available at: <https://businessgraphics.com.br/wp-content/uploads/2020/12/CULTURAESCOLA-E-PROCESSOS-FORMATIVOS-EM-EDUCACAO.pdf> Acessed on: 30 mar. 2023. Free Translation.

possibilities for analysis. Such reordering allowed us to go beyond what becomes effective as an immediate solution, requiring continuing reflection for real media and technological literacy.

Listening to teachers also allowed us a different perspective. Starting from dialogue presupposes interactive listening to reflect on educational praxis, which guided this work's proposal and integrated the Graduate course that gave rise to the walk. Ribeiro[12] indicates that all paths taken allow us to understand the actual place of speech. In this research, we used the participants' thinking to understand their standpoints, places of speech, comprehension of the topic, and weaknesses that derive from this.

The different readings necessary to understand the world, according to Freire[13], bring the need for a critical, open, and radical posture, which remodels the teaching performance. Internalizing multiple readings about technology and their use in the educational process collaborates with the continuing education of teachers, enabling these professionals to deepen their knowledge and consciously use such mechanisms.

Indeed, the pandemic period was a challenge and a troubled moment for teachers and students, leaving sequels in student learning. Still, it also aroused several concerns, among which the fundamental role of the school and the necessary and uncontestable character of face-to-face

---

12 Ribeiro, D. O que é o lugar da fala? Letramento: Justificando. Belo Horizonte, 2017.
13 Freire, P. Pedagogia da esperança: um reencontro com a pedagogia do oprimido. Paz e Terra: Rio de Janeiro, 1997.

teaching for Basic education. There is a strong need for continuing education regarding the use of educational technologies for better performance, considering that this will be the course for the coming years, bearing in mind that the insertion of technologies, despite being fragmented, directs the walk in the didactic, school, pedagogical scope.

Continuing teacher education needs permanent dialogue, active listening, and attention to these teachers' standpoints and places of speech[14]. We need educational processes that do not have their quality evaluated by immediatism, and that do not use technologies solely in marketing and instrumental ways. Faced with such a scenario, it is up to us to emphasize that such questions are essential for debates so that the permanent construction of a conscious educational process, which seeks constant reflection on the part of our teachers and students, is possible.

---

14   Ribeiro, D. O que é o lugar da fala? Letramento: Justificando. Belo Horizonte, 2017.

7

Listening in academic processes:
supervisor/supervisee relationship in Graduate Education

Najara Escarião Agripino

Abstract

The present study results from the final work produced under the course "**Listening, Curiosity and Love**" from the Federal University of Rio de Janeiro's Graduate Program in History of Sciences, Techniques and Epistemology. It is characterized as field research with a qualitative approach, and its main objective is to investigate the perception of graduate students during the dissertation development phase about listening in the supervision process. A questionnaire and semi-structured interviews – applied via WhatsApp – were used as data collection instruments. Fourteen students were heard. The findings indicate that most students are aligned with their supervisors and have ease in the process of guiding their work, while a smaller part of the students reported alignment difficulties: they felt invalidated as researchers, excluded from the process of defining the research topic, and demonstrated problems in establishing dialogues and beings listened. It was concluded that, although technical skills and academic affinity are important for supervisees according to the international literature, the personal characteristics of supervisors, such as ease in establishing dialogue and listening, were identified as the factors with the greatest impact from the perspective of master's students about the development of work and feelings about graduate studies.

Keywords: Listening. Postgraduate studies. Academic Supervision

Introduction

Entering graduate school at the master's and/or doctoral level is an achievement that has countless implications for the newcomer's life and requires sacrifices and changes in routines. In a brief review of the literature, it appears that much has been said about stress in graduate studies, both from the perspective of students, professors, and other technical professionals. However, research that investigates aspects involving supervision processes, as well as the relationships between supervisor and supervisees, are still not very expressive.

According to Brolezzi[1] supervisors are subjects who interact in a unique, intersubjective, and complex way with their supervisees, and it is from these relationships that a large part of a country's academic production derives. However, this productivity is linked to the condition of establishing a favorable and effective relationship for the generation of knowledge. For this reason, the author assumes that, by renouncing their functions, the actors can cause ruptures in this relationship, negatively influencing the construction process and the quality of the works. It is observed that the knowledge construction process is not an individual activity, but rather a collaborative endeavor between the professor and the student.

A study carried out by Leite Filho and Martins[2],

---

[1] BROLEZZI, A. C. Empatia na Relação Aluno/Professor/Conhecimento. Revista de Psicologia, v. 17, n. 27, p. 1-21, 2014.

[2] LEITE FILHO, G. A.; MARTINS, G. A. Relação orientador-orientando e suas influências na elaboração de teses e dissertações. Rev. Administração de Empresas, v. 46 (Ed. Esp.), 99-109, 2006. doi: 10.1590/S0034-75902006000500008.

with graduate students in accounting at the University of São Paulo, PUC-SP and FECAP (all in Brazil), identified that supervisors tend to value technical characteristics of supervisees in the application process, while supervisees value affective and personal characteristics of the supervisors. Furthermore, the study indicates that the lack of systematization, support, feedback, and the autocracy of the environment inflict feelings of anguish, insecurity, and loneliness on the supervisees.

One can see the lack of guidance on the part of supervisees to share their fears and insecurity with their supervisors, while at the same time seeking support from these professors to complete an important and decisive stage in their academic trajectories. It is at this point that listening is identified as a necessary teaching practice to re-signify the teacher-supervisor and teacher-researcher roles, since the objective of this relationship should not be restricted to academic aspects, but also to promote a more humane and conduction to the full development of knowledge.

Listening as a teaching practice tends to facilitate dialogue in the teacher/student relationship, since, by placing the latter at the center of relationships, it provides greater understanding of the individual and consequently contributes to their learning. By reducing the asymmetry of the relationship's hierarchy, responsibilities can be shared, making the process more dynamic, collaborative, and motivational, whenever they are willing to dialogue and listen.

It is true that professors, in general, are not trained to listen, and they are also charged for productivity and performance, often not being available to interact qualitatively with their students. Given the difficulties faced by both professors and graduate students, this text presents the following guiding problems: What is the importance of listening in the graduate supervision process? What is the perception of graduate students about listening to by their supervisors?

Based on the questions, the research objective is to investigate the perception of graduate students in the dissertation development phase about by being listened to by their supervisors in the research supervision process. The work is organized into theoretical notes, which address the supervisor-student relationship in graduate school and listening as a pedagogical practice. Then, the methodological paths are presented, advancing to the presentation and discussion of the results, ending with the last considerations.

Theoretical notes

Academic supervision is the main stage of the pedagogical relationship established between supervisor and supervisee throughout graduate school, and it is a process that, although its general characteristics are dynamic and interpersonal relationships, has singularities and subjectivities in each established interpersonal relationship, and will be established at different levels[3].

In his research on the subject, Armstrong[4] discussed the effects of the actors' cognitive and interpersonal profile on the quality of graduate supervision processes and concluded that success depends on predominant factors, namely: standards and skills of communication, interactivity pattern, honesty, ability to exert influence, loyal subordination, empathy, intelligence, respect, personality, mutual obligation, politeness, and dominance. This time, the supervisor-supervisee interaction would be inserted in a much broader perspective than the academic one, encompassing discussions about human relationships.

At the same time, the study carried out by Rodrigues, Fleith and Alves[5] indicated conditioning elements that promote interactions of an academic and non-academic nature in this relationship, with those of an academic nature: academic affinity, preparation, interest, academic formalities, academic rituals, and competence in the field, and those of a non-academic nature: personal affinity, availability of time, and personal problems.

Unlike other teaching and learning processes in higher education, graduate supervision is not limited to the proper production of a dissertation or thesis, but also to

---

3 VIANA, C. M. Q. Q.; VEIGA, I. P. A. O diálogo acadêmico entre orientadores e orientandos. Educação, v. 33, n. 3, p. 222-226, 2010.

4 ARMSTRONG, S. J. The impact of supervisors' cognitive styles on the quality of research supervision in management education. British Journal of Educational Psychology, v. 74, n. 4, p. 599-616, 2004. doi: 10.1348/0007099042376436.

5 RODRIGUES JÚNIOR, J. F.; FLEITH, D. S.; ALVES, K. M. B. A dissertação de mestrado: um estudo sobre as interações entre o orientador e o orientando com base em incidentes críticos. Revista Brasileira de Estudos Pedagógicos, v. 74, n. 177, p. 437-463, 1993. doi: 10.24109/2176-6681.rbep.74i177.1205.

training students as independent researchers[6].

Viana and Veiga[7] add that supervision success depends on dialogue, dedication, organization, discipline, interest, and satisfaction, associated with the commitment and responsibility of both, requiring self-assessment of the parties.

In turn, Valente, Almeida and Geraldini[8] draw attention to the importance of using new methodologies as pedagogical strategies to place students at the center of the teaching and learning process, changing the traditionally imposed order by the pedagogical models that had the teacher's figure as the focus of the educational process.

It should be noted that the practice of listening can be seen as a new active teaching-learning method, since education becomes more centered on the student and guides learning in the perspectives, experiences and needs of the student, adapting the academic supervision process to the profile of each graduate student.

Methodological path

The study is based on field research with a qualitative approach and included graduate students in Administration

---

6   GRANT, B. Mapping the pleasures and risks of supervision. Discourse, v. 24, n. 2, p. 175-190, 2003. doi: 10.1080/01596300303042.

7   VIANA, C. M. Q. Q.; VEIGA, I. P. A. O diálogo acadêmico entre orientadores e orientandos. Educação, v. 33, n. 3, p. 222-226, 2010.

8   VALENTE, V. A.; ALMEIDA, M. E. B.; GERALDINI, A. F. S. Metodologias Ativas: das concepções às práticas em distintos níveis de ensino. Revista Diálogo Educacional, v. 17, n. 52, p. 455-478, 2017.

(master's level) - from a federal university located in the city of Campina Grande, Paraíba, Brazil, in the development phase of their master's thesis.

The study was guided by ethical research standards, with the guarantee of voluntary participation, anonymity (we adopted pseudonyms to ensure confidentiality), and the right to withdraw. Twenty students of the program in the qualification/defense phase were approached. After explaining the procedures, one of them withdrew from participating because he claimed to be emotionally shaken by his graduate experience, not being able to talk about his relationship with the supervisor. Five claimed a lack of time for the interview, leaving us with fourteen students with a profile for the study.

Data collection took place in two stages: the first was the application of a questionnaire through the Google Forms platform, with the objective of tracing the profile and academic situation of the researched population. The second consisted of a semi-structured interview, also carried out online, through Whatsapp application, between February 7 and 13, 2023, with five master's students in the qualification phase and nine master's students in the thesis defense phase.

The research took place remotely, since some of the graduate students were in cities and even states far from the university where they are enrolled, thus making face-to-face contact unfeasible.

The interviews were conducted by audio and lasted

an average of fifteen minutes. The script was prepared based on the researcher's experiences with graduate school and on the dialogues throughout the discipline "**Listening, Curiosity and Love**".

Table 1 presents the interviewees' profile.

Table 1 - Profile of Research Participants

Participants	Age Range	Occupation	Scholarship	Phase
Pedro	26-35	Just studies	Throughout the master's	Defense
Ana	32-37	works and studies	No	Defense
Carol	32-37	Just studies	Throughout the master's	Defense
Iza	32-37	works and studies	No	Defense
Erica	44-49	works and studies	No	Defense
Francisca	44-49	works and studies	No	Defense
Rita	26-31	Just studies	Throughout the master's	Qualification
Laura	32-37	works and studies	No	Qualification
Leticia	26-31	Just studies	Throughout the master's	Qualification
John	32-37	works and studies	No	Qualification
Junior	26-31	works and studies	During the first year of the Master's	Defense
Alison	26-31	Just studies	No	Qualification
Stele	26-32	works and studies	During the first year of the Master's	recently defended
Monica	26-31	Just studies	No	recently defended

Source: Survey data (2023).

As shown in Table 1, the survey covered only students who had completed the program credits and were in the process of preparing their thesis. Two of the interviewed students had recently defended their theses and still had an institutional link; only four were full scholarship holders.

For the interview stage, a script with five questions was applied, which were organized into academic categories: academic affinity; and of a non-academic nature: dialogue, listening and job satisfaction. The categories were defined based on the literature. The aim was to relate the students' perception of listening in academic supervision with job satisfaction and research training.

The analysis of the results follows the structure

proposed by Bardin[9], which is organized in three stages: 1) pre-analysis; 2) material exploration, categorization, or coding; 3) treatment of results, inferences, and interpretation. The research categories were analyzed individually, confronting the responses of graduate students with the literature on the subject.

Presentation and discussion of the results

We sought to identify some important aspects of students' academic trajectories, such as requests for time extensions and supervision changes. Data were obtained in the initial stage of the research, with the application of the questionnaire and are shown in Table 2.

Among the fourteen interviewees, four requested a deadline extension, one of them due to emotional issues that compromised productivity. No participant requested a change of supervisor, but six considered this possibility and the main reason was lack of alignment.

---

9   BARDIN, L. Análise de conteúdo. São Paulo: Edições 70, 2011.

Table 2 - Academic situation of the participants

Participants	Requested extension	Thought about a supervisor change
Pedro	No	No
Ana	No	No
Carol	No	"Yes. Because sometimes I feel insecure"
Iza	No	"I felt a little lonely, sometimes a little lost. I saw that other colleagues received more support and I thought that, assisted by another supervisor, I could improve my performance."
Erica	No	No
Francisca	Yes, due to difficulties in data collection	"I would change because I thought the way of guiding could be different. But the change process is more difficult than staying [with the same supervisor]"
Rita	No	No
Laura	No	No
Leticia	No	"Yes, due to my supervisor not giving me enough attention"
John	No	"Yes, to enter a research line that was closer [to my interests]"
Junior	Yes, due to difficulties in research development, supervision, and loss of scholarship	"I thought about not being able to develop what was aligned and realized that I could have been better guided by another supervisor".
Alison	No	No
Stele	Yes, due to illness	No
Monica	Yes, difficulties in data collection	No

Source: Own elaboration (2023).

Academic categories

Initially, we questioned about the academic affinity with the supervisor. Verifying the existence of academic affinity between the parties is important to identify variables that could compromise the dialogue between those involved.

Although most students reported good rapport, three of them (Junior, João and Francisca) said they did not, which is one of the reasons for dissatisfaction with the graduate program. It is worth mentioning that of the students who stated that they did not have an academic affinity with their supervisor, two needed a deadline extension (Junior and Francisca) and all of them thought about changing supervisors. We highlight here the speech of Junior, who is in the extension period for defense:

> *[...] at first it seemed that the theme was similar, right? The research proposal with my research idea. But then I realized that the research idea would perhaps be more worked on, and better understood by a specific supervisor on the topic I went to work on. Because, actually, the idea was to do more quantitative, more detailed research, and when developing this study, right? [...], this project was not taking the paths that were aligned with the supervisor's, or also with what I proposed, and because it had this favorable performance neither for one side nor for the other, maybe this affinity was not so clear (Junior).*

Based on the student's perception, the lack of affinity with the supervisor made a theme that was thought to be common among the parties become a point of divergence, since the work directions were confusing for both. The main point of divergence would have been the structure and choice of methodological procedures. Oliveira[10] clarifies that satisfaction with supervision, as well as the quality of interactions with the supervisor, can be improved once there is cognitive similarity between both. It is important to emphasize the willingness to adapt to the other and try to seek points of convergence to overcome differences.

Non-academic categories

According to Severino[11], supervision is a process that requires dialogical interaction between those involved, in which all forms of submission or oppression are abolished. This time, we sought to better understand this relationship,

---

10 OLIVEIRA, A. S. Relação Orientador-Orientando e a Teoria das Relações Interpessoais de Robert Hinde. 130 f. Dissertação (Mestrado em Educação), Universidade Católica de Brasília, 2006.

11 SEVERINO, A. J. Metodologia do Trabalho Científico. 22 ed. São Paulo: Cortez, 2002.

questioning the supervisees about their perception of the dialogue with their supervisors.

Nine of the interviewees reported establishing a good dialogue with their supervisors, as highlighted in Letícia's speech:

> [...] the dialogue I have with her is only during meetings, and sometimes informally outside meeting hours. But so, when we have a dialogue, I have all my doubts cleared and she supervises me (Letícia).

The speeches of Letícia and others clarify that the relationship is good, but restricted to work supervision, with no personal involvement.

For master's students Iza, Carol, João, Francisca and Junior, although there is an openness to dialogue and a good relationship with their supervisors, there are reservations related to conversation and listening, as expressed by Iza:

> So, I found it more challenging in the beginning because I was extremely lost, I didn't have a very exact notion of what was expected of me as a researcher in this master's process and... sometimes I had, for example, doubt about a methodological question, and... it kind of passed me this need to run after, to seek... and it was not that I didn't want to do it, but I missed that direction a little, [...], it seemed to me be a bit of an abandonment, right? [...]. Another challenge that I think is very big is [...] regarding listening, sometimes I would start to defend an idea about my work, and before I said the first ten words, she [the supervisor] already had a ready answer and already... sometimes she dropped what I was going to say and when she finished the argument I said: 'because that's not what I was going to talk about, so, let me say what I would like to say, so that later we can analyze whether it is viable or not?'. So we have this bit of difficulty. [...] and we know that this interferes a little with the listening process (Iza).

According to Iza, the most difficult phase of this process was establishing the initial dialogue and defining a research proposal, the same issue raised by Junior, João, Francisca and Carol. For these researchers, finding a common theme of interest and having their ideas about conducting research accepted by their supervisors was a difficult and unsatisfactory process, which led them to even consider a supervisor change.

Although Armstrong[12] considers that the technical aspects are more important for the supervisees than the personal factors of this relationship, for these students the personal characteristics of the advisers, such as ease in establishing dialogue and listening, also interfered with both the research development and about their feelings towards graduate school. For these three master's students, even though they were working on a common topic of interest with their supervisors, they still did not feel fully heard or considered in this process.

The study also sought to verify the perception of supervisees about being listened to by their supervisors. Most of the students evaluated the listening process positively. João and Junior, for example, indicated that after overcoming the initial difficulties of dialogue, listening during supervision became satisfactory throughout the research, indicating that the greatest difficulty for them was in academic affinity, which interfered with the dialogue between the parts. Master's students Estela, Carol, and Iza

---

[12] ARMSTRONG, S. J. The impact of supervisors' cognitive styles on the quality of research supervision in management education. British Journal of Educational Psychology, v. 74, n. 4, p. 599-616, 2004. doi: 10.1348/0007099042376436.

reinforced difficulties related to choosing the study proposal and autonomy in the research development process:

> In relation to that [listening] I was quite, yeah... I was quite like that... plastered [sigh]. Because she already had it, right? the... the theme... like, that she wanted me to write. [...] how she proposed the theme to me [...], so I just followed it, you know? And when I had doubts, she answered with... with... like that, with clarity. So I... I didn't really have this issue of... yeah... of doubt... of... like, my position is different from hers... because it was kind of what I was [sic] [...] following her position (Estela).

Thus, although the supervisor's proposal prevailed in most of the process, Estela claims to have agreed and understood her supervisor's proposal as a better alternative for carrying out the work. However, she considered that she was not much heard and that she had little protagonism regarding decisions related to her thesis. Students Carol and Iza gave a similar response.

Still regarding the students who indicated that they felt little considered/heard in the supervision process, only Carol and Iza considered a supervisor change. For them, not only the lack of listening but general dialogue difficulties with their supervisors aroused a feeling of insecurity regarding work quality and the support received to develop the research.

It is important to note that during the interview, Junior expressed dissatisfaction with the work supervision several times, but it was clear that the difficulty was in academic affinity and not in dialogue and listening:

> Whenever I put how I thought... what it should be... yeah... my supervisor, she... complied, right? She always tried to

allow me to develop research on something I was familiar with, right? to help in the process (Junior).

To Moura and Giannela[13] listening is a social and dialogical act that "requires openness to recognize that the other is the possible source of a differentiated perception and has something to contribute (in the learning process, in the management of organizations, public policies, etc.). In this sense, we can assume a passive and/or welcoming attitude". The authors add that listening facilitates collective work and organization processes, effectively establishing capacities for creative inquiry, divergent thinking, and exploration of new options and non-obvious possibilities.

Based on Moura and Giannela[14] and considering the testimonies of nine students in the graduate program, it is possible to consider that most teachers adopt a positive attitude regarding listening to their supervisees and establishing partnerships in this process. On the other hand, the other five supervisors were pointed out by their supervisees as paying little attention to the dialogue and preferences of the supervisees.

The understanding that the development of a thesis/dissertation is a double effort - sometimes a trio - is essential for a good relationship between the parties. However, as a recurrent behavior in graduate studies, some supervisors still take advantage of their supervisees to carry out research of their personal interest, disregarding the researcher's identity

---

[13] MOURA, M. S. S.; GIANNELA, V. A arte de escutar: nuances de um campo de práticas e de conhecimento. Revista Terceiro Incluído, v. 6, p. 9-24, 2016, p. 10. doi: 10.5216/teri.v6i1.40739. Free translation.

[14] Idem.

and the supervisee's choices about their work.

Supervisees were asked how they assess the importance of listening in the supervision process. All graduate students consider it to be of paramount importance for efficient and satisfactory development.

> [...] I think it's very important, so, from the beginning, to have the first contact already during the first semester, trying to do the maximum with the supervisor to do the mentoring process, because... what I realize... when we get to the master's, especially if we're already leaving an undergraduate program and entering the master's, it's... there's a lack of understanding of how things work [sic], right? and... As the supervisor, the professor, he is ahead of the student... of that master's proposal, he should shape the student's profile, I see it that way. So it's like a mentor. There was supposed to be this mentoring process, right? to customize the student there. Yeah... I don't know how to talk about the case, like... people who already come from other programs, who already have a master's degree... I'm talking about the specific case of someone who is leaving graduation, as in my case (Junior).

According to Junior's perception, it is important to foster dialogue throughout the work development process, but especially when entering the graduate program and making initial decisions about the research, to avoid dissatisfaction and even a feeling of abandonment.

Entering graduate school is usually the moment when students are most vulnerable and in need of follow-up to define their research interests and identities as researchers.

As for the main difficulty faced during the thesis development, the interviewees pointed out the time limitation and personal lives, in the sense of reconciling the master's degree with the work or family routine: only Junior, João, Francisca and Letícia pointed out the supervision:

> At the moment it's [...] being in relation to supervision, because I'm [...] getting little guidance. But even so, when I have it, it clears my doubts, but even so, I don't think much, you know? In a sense, because she has many things to [...] do, many supervisees to guide, then sometimes... when we schedule a meeting, sometimes we cancel it due to another appointment, you know? These little things like that. Then the person is... trying to set up a meeting with her every week and sometimes they cancel, you know? The only problem is this. [...] My biggest difficulty is time, because she doesn't have much time to give guidance, the necessary support [...] (Letícia).

For the other master's students, as well as for Laura, the greatest difficulty has been in reconciling the routine with the dedication time needed for the master's activities:

> As I'm still [sic] in the very beginning, my biggest difficulty has not been in relation to the supervisor. My biggest difficulty has been in relation to myself, I'm [sic] in the systematic literature review phase and it's a phase... it's... extremely tiring, meticulous. And as I, in addition to doing a master's degree, work and have a young son, my time is reduced. So, this has been my biggest difficulty, it has nothing to do with supervision, but with myself (Laura).

Although it is not the objective of this work to discuss the student's personal and academic relationships and the pressures imposed, above all, on women in a double (sometimes triple) journey of reconciling domestic/family tasks with graduate attributions, Laura's speech opens an important parenthesis. According to Haynes and Fearfull[15]

---

[15] HAYNES, K.; FEARFULL, A. Exploring ourselves: Exploiting and resisting gendered identities of women academics in accounting and management. Pacific Accounting Review, v. 20, n. 2, p. 185–204, 2008. doi: 10.1108/01140580810892508.

and to Cherkowski and Bosetti[16], the need to reconcile academic identities with personal demands can, in most cases, generate tension, fatigue and even depression in female students subjected to heavy workloads. Laura, as well as other students in the program, manages a work, study, and family routine, which can compromise her satisfaction with the work and dialogue with her supervisor throughout the process, as well as adding even more stress to the mental load of graduate women students, a situation made worse by sanitary measures during the Covid-19 pandemic.

> *The difficulty I had was with the issue of time, right? To reconcile the master's degree with work and with the pandemic issue, which we lost, right? This direct contact there at the university, which also hinders, I think it disturbed everyone, it's... even writing, concentrating and everything else. Yeah, because of all that and, yeah... because of... difficulties, right? That I went through, I do not consider the work satisfactory. Because I could have been much, much better. What was lacking is... there was a lack of engagement, both on my part and on her part, from the supervisor (Estela).*

Estela makes it clear in her speech how the stress caused by the accumulation of responsibilities, aggravated by the pandemic, interfered with her motivation and satisfaction with her work, an argument also presented by Carol.

For a better understanding of satisfaction with the research, the study sought to find out how master's students feel about their work. According to responses, ten of the students considered themselves satisfied with their

---

[16] CHERKOWSKI, S.; BOSETTI, L. Behind the veil: Academic women negotiating demands of femininity. Women's Studies International Forum, v. 45, p. 19–26, 2014. doi: 10.1016/j.wsif.2014.03.013.

research, while four declared some dissatisfaction.

> *Regarding the direction of the research, it was not what I expected. [...]. Yeah... the supervisor's idea was to do it in the model of three articles. At first, I thought it was very good, I wanted to do it in three articles, but at the same time I also wanted it to be in the model of one article, the traditional model because I thought it would be a little easier, right? But because I like challenges, I still agreed, I accepted, right? But it wasn't as I expected and even because now in overtime, we're going to try to do the traditional model, right? [...] I think what could have improved in the master's degree would be the selection of the supervisor... that the collegiate had the zeal there when deciding... according to the supervisor's specialty for that proposal of the supervisee... as much as possible try to understand the proposal of what the mentee wants to do. Because sometimes it indicates a mentor who cannot understand or help the mentee. So, this can cause dissatisfaction and even drop out of graduate school (Junior).*

> *In that sense of work satisfaction, no. Another thing, which was very complicated, was the qualification issue because one of the teachers was extremely... rude! And that kind of stopped me from continuing to write about the topic... I kind of stayed... blocked, you know? The theme. Given the way he, yeah... exposed me on the day. So, all this culminated in dissatisfaction in the end, you know? With the work. Demotivation, you know? (Stela).*

Dissatisfied respondents pointed out the lack of identification with the carried-out research or with the chosen methods, as pointed out by Junior. Estela, in turn, in addition to the lack of identification, alleged trauma during the qualification, when a member of the committee used harsh words to analyze her project. For Estela, not only dissatisfaction with work supervision, but dissatisfaction with the master's experience itself influenced her perception of graduate studies.

Allinson, Armstrong and Hayes[17] consider that the supervisors' cognitive styles can significantly impact the guidance process. This was confirmed in our research.

Conclusion

Academic supervision, in addition to being a mandatory graduate school component, encompasses the establishment of human relationships and, like all human interactions, is complex and subject to emotions and feelings. After hearing and analyzing fourteen master's students, the research findings converged in some respects with the literature on the subject. Although technical issues such as knowledge and academic affinity are fundamental for work development, the personal aspects of this relationship were the ones that most positively and negatively impacted academic supervision in the view of the investigated master's students.

For nine of the fourteen students interviewed, academic affinity and being listened to by their supervisors contributed to work satisfaction. Two students - who claimed not to have an academic affinity with their supervisors – considered that the ease of dialogue and listening helped them get around the situation and overcome the initial difficulties. For Francisca, who also pointed out a lack of

---

[17] ALLINSON, C. W.; ARMSTRONG, S. J.; HAYES, J. Formal Mentoring Systems: An Examination of the Effects of Mentor/Protégé Cognitive Styles on the Mentoring Process. Journal of Management Studies, v. 39, n. 8, p. 1111-1132, dez. 2002. doi: 10.1111/1467-6486.00326.

academic affinity, the research line, divergences regarding the work vision and dialogue difficulties represented points of dissatisfaction with the supervision process that persisted until the final phase of the thesis elaboration.

As for the two students who considered that their views on the work were not considered, even though there was academic affinity and points of convergence with their supervisors, the feeling of invalidation compromised the relationship and satisfaction with the final thesis result.

It is understood that dialogue and listening, especially when entering graduate school, and initial decisions about the research, both directly interfered with work satisfaction and feelings about the master's degree. Specifically, regarding listening, students who did not consider themselves heard demonstrated dissatisfaction and even frustration with the production of their theses, feeling invalidated in their identities as researchers.

Attention is drawn to the passive posture of dissatisfied students, who, despite considering the possibility of changing their supervisors, decided to remain with them instead of seeking to solve the problem. This leads us to question whether, in fact, there was no space for the supervisors to listen, or whether the master's students did not know how to make themselves heard, preferring self-indulgence to protagonism in carrying out the research.

It was also seen that academic affinity alone is not enough to conduct a good supervision process, while the absence of good dialogue, empathetic listening and not knowing how to make oneself heard are directly related to dissatisfaction in the supervisor-student relationship.

It is concluded, then, that even with academic affinity, when there is no listening, supervision can be an ineffective and even demotivating process. This time, academic affinity combined with good communication are fundamental for the development of graduate research. And both parties must be committed to good dialogue.

As contributions, this study brings a critical reflection on an important and neglected aspect in graduate studies, when discussing the personal and non-academic aspects that affect relationships in academic supervision. As for limitations and future research, we only considered students who remained in the master's program until completion, excluding dropout students. Research can consider dropouts as a range of possibilities for analyzing dialogue and listening and their impacts on the academic trajectory of this group.

8

Considerations on the construction of this tool-book

Igor Vinicius Lima Valentim

Listening, curiosity, and love, as a graduate course with master's and PhD students, was taught with the combination of three aspects: synchronous online/remote mode, active learning methods, and educational principles towards more loving interpersonal relationships.

In this book, we share some wonderful productions derived from this exercise of educational experimentation and, at the same time, a lot of dedication, excellence, and sensitivity.

It is no exaggeration to say that **Listening, curiosity, and love** only existed because of the courage of many people who accepted the adventure and challenge with great rigor, dedication, work, and... joy! In the same way, this book was only possible because the university stepped outside of its walls and the students and professor agreed to experiment. Jumped the walls of the ivory tower.

Even if only momentarily, the conservative university opened itself to other cities, other states, other regions, other accents, other voices and sensibilities, different areas of knowledge, different life stories and backgrounds in a giant country like Brazil: an infinite, diverse, multiple power combined!

After completing the course and presenting the final individual works, some people showed interest in using their products as raw material for the construction of texts so that they could be shared in the form of a book. The final products included videos, performances, slideshows, poems, letters, mini documentaries, as well as a few texts in the traditional academic article format. From this desire, we built a group with those who wanted to produce this new product, now a book chapter, based on what each had developed for the graduate course, but at this point, no longer directly linked to it (the course had already been closed and grading process finalized).

The most interesting thing seemed to be the production of a book with a well-articulated and organically constructed guiding thread. We had several meetings in which each student read the productions of all the others, from the abstracts to the final texts. Opined. Brought suggestions. After a few months, all texts were revised at least twice, and the organization of the book continued.

It is possible to use remote teaching courses that are tuition-free and open to students from all over Brazil, simultaneously with the full use of active learning methods to enhance authorial, creative, and quality students' products, with much more work and dedication needed and involved.

Do we want this?

Changing learning methods will not solve all education problems. But it's a step. One step. It's no use working with active learning methods while we continue to think we own the truth, unique and unquestionable, or in search of it. Curiosity, listening, and love do not combine with unique and unquestionable truths.

This book is an immense source of joy and pleasure, as Roberto Freire[1] said, a sign that it is possible to do things differently, to walk differently, to build different things, even with all the difficulties that come with experimentation and development of the new.

We challenge ourselves, in Graduate Education, in Masters's and Doctoral courses, to dare. Without expositive classes, without just reading and debating texts (although we have done this a lot to serve as tools), we wanted to build something that would make sense for students, for the teacher, and to produce a different society, even taking a lot more work from all of us.

There is no transformative education that is possible (in the direction of the society that we desire) if it is based on people's sadness, hierarchy, and submission.

Sharing experiences such as those present in this book also has the purpose of serving as a source of encouragement for those who are restless. For the restless men and women of universities in the 21st century. For those who don't want to continue reproducing various medieval academic modes of functioning and various medieval academic relationships. May this book serve as a

---

[1] FREIRE, R. Sem tesão não há solução. 20. ed. São Paulo: Trigrama, 1990.

tool and stimulus.

We often feel alone.

We don't always have institutional support.

We don't always have support from our own colleagues.

But we are not alone.

We need to get to know each other, listen to each other, read each other, exchange experiences, and build changes in our daily lives towards the worlds that make our eyes shine and fill us with joy and lust.

No matter how small they are.
The texts that make up this book are living proof that it is possible.

Index

A

abandonment 116, 120

ability 41, 84, 109

academia 23, 43-44, 46-48, 57-58

academic 17-19, 24, 31-34, 40-41, 44, 48, 56-57, 64, 79, 103, 105-115, 117-118, 121-122, 124-126, 130-131

acceptance 52, 54, 57

achievement 54, 106

activities 16, 19-21, 26-28, 65, 67, 89, 121

administration 35, 37-39, 43-56, 58, 110

adversities 78, 85

affect 42, 57, 126

affection 34, 70

affinity 67, 105, 109, 112, 114-115, 117-118, 124-126

alertness 90

alignment 46, 105, 113

alternatives 24-25, 68, 80, 84

analysis 43-44, 51, 55, 100, 112-113

anger 81

anguish 107

Anthroposophy 64, 66

anxieties 64, 82

approach 43, 61, 67, 69, 91, 93, 105, 110

art 61-62, 65, 67, 92-93

asymmetry 107

attention 26, 45, 48, 90, 101, 110, 119, 125

attitude 52-53, 119

author 40-42, 46, 55, 61, 63, 78-79, 81, 86, 106

authorship 27

autocracy 107

autoethnography 24

autonomy 27, 31, 65, 68-69, 118

B

beginning 32, 62, 84, 116, 120-121

behavior 42, 75, 119

bitterness 31

Bourdieu 40

Brazil 15-18, 20, 23, 25, 31, 33, 39, 55, 61, 64-65, 68, 70-71, 75-77, 82, 89, 92, 107, 111, 129-130

C

care 42, 75, 77

challenge 31-33, 41-42, 50, 56, 58, 99-100, 116, 129, 131

changes 22, 55, 61-62, 75-77, 81-84, 106, 113, 132

character 62, 90-91, 98, 100

children 65, 67-68, 70, 79-80

choice 42-43, 83, 90, 115

clandestine 19

classes 21, 25-28, 32, 47-48, 50, 131

classroom 26, 32, 92, 96-97

collaborative 31, 106-107

colleagues 17, 53-54, 132

collegiate 68, 123

comfort 80

commitment 26, 28, 42, 110

committee 123

commodification 55

communication 54, 89, 109, 126

community 37, 39, 70-71

competence 99, 109

competition 40, 42

computer 49

concerns 39, 43, 80, 100

conditions 38, 50-51, 53, 56, 76-77, 96

context 15, 19, 77, 83, 89, 91

conversation 75, 116

Coronavírus 82

courage 61, 76, 129

course 15-17, 20-23, 26, 29, 31-34, 37-38, 48, 52, 54, 79, 90, 100-101, 105, 129-130

covid-19 17, 75-76, 78-79, 81-85, 99, 122

creation 16, 61

creative 20, 119, 130

creativity 27

crisis 82

criteria 46

critical 25, 48, 69, 78, 89-93, 97-100, 126

criticism 41

culture 40-41, 46, 93

curiosity 13, 15-19, 21-22, 24-25, 27, 29, 32, 37-38, 45, 61-64, 66, 70, 75, 78-79, 89-90, 105, 112, 129, 131

curriculum 66, 71

cynicism 41

Index

135

D

data   37, 39, 78, 105, 111, 113

decision-making   68

dedication   19, 21, 23, 26, 28, 70, 110, 121, 129-130

defense   111, 114

degree 38-39, 120-123, 125

democratization   96-97

denialism   82

depression   122

desire   20, 26, 33, 41, 45, 64, 66, 78, 130-131

despair 83

development   16, 22, 27, 39, 52, 65, 69, 79, 91, 105, 107-108, 111, 117-120, 124, 126, 131

diasporas   73, 76, 78-79, 83

differences   115

difficulties   22, 48, 50-51, 53, 76, 80, 83, 105, 108, 117-118, 122, 124-125, 131

digital   86, 89, 93, 99

dilemmas   82

discipline   21, 31, 61, 110, 112

discourse   42, 56, 110

disinterest   25

dissatisfaction 38, 68, 114, 118, 120, 123, 125-126

dissertation   38, 64, 105, 108-109, 119

divergence   115

diversity   20-21, 28, 33, 44, 48, 51, 68, 93

dreams 27-28, 64, 82

dropout   126

E

education   13, 15, 19, 23-28, 31, 39, 46, 54-55, 57, 61, 64-65, 67, 69-71, 77, 83, 87, 89, 91-92, 94-95, 97-101, 103, 109-110, 117, 130-131

educators   33, 89, 91, 95, 98-99

effects 81, 109, 124

effort   27, 119

elections   83

emotions   81, 85, 124

empathy   61, 75, 109

encounters   15, 20, 23

engagement   122

enrollment   17-18

ethics   24, 42, 45-46

etymology   78

evaluation   65

exams   22

exchanges   21, 23, 55-56, 80, 90, 98

existence   18, 83, 114

expectations   33

experiences   26-27, 31-32, 67, 110, 112, 131-132

experiential 80
experiment 61, 129
experimentation 15, 129, 131
exploration 55, 113, 119
extension 113-114

F

faculty 18-19, 25, 28
failure 41, 57
fatigue 122
fear 76, 82
feelings 81, 85, 105, 107, 117, 124-125
fieldwork 20, 27
finitude 76, 81
formation 62, 70
freedom 31, 44, 69
Freire 25, 37, 41, 69, 78, 85, 90, 92, 100, 131
frustration 46-47, 125

G

gender 48
government 75, 80, 83
governmentality 40
grading 18, 130
graduation 91, 120
growth 63, 70, 97

H

hands-on 21
happy 33-34, 69, 84-85
harassment 24
health 76-77, 81
hierarchy 68, 107, 131
humankind 70

I

idea 25, 48, 57, 115-116, 123
ideologies 98
idolatry 23
impact 19, 70, 81, 105, 109, 117, 124
improvement 54, 57
inaction 83
incentive 20
income 51, 76-77, 92
inequalities 77
innovation 49
in-person 26, 95
insecurity 31, 107, 118
integrity 42
intelligence 109
interaction 43, 91, 93, 99, 109, 115
interdisciplinary 49
interfaces 65
international 105, 122

Index

interview 111-112, 118

involvement 19, 26, 116

isolation 18

J

journey 33-34, 48-49, 56, 62, 64, 121

joy 24, 28, 61, 129, 131-132

justice 46

K

knowledge 16, 18-20, 23, 25, 28, 31, 33-34, 37-42, 44-45, 48-50, 53, 55, 58, 68-69, 79, 90, 99-100, 106-107, 124, 129

L

learning 15-16, 20-24, 26, 28, 32-33, 59, 61-62, 65, 68, 70, 90-91, 93, 95-98, 100, 107, 109-110, 119, 129-130

lectures 21

leisure 98

life 20, 27, 31, 34, 40-42, 48, 53, 55, 65, 71, 75-77, 84, 106, 129

limitations 44, 55, 126

limits 45, 98

listen 22, 32, 39, 89, 107-108, 125, 132

listening 13, 15-19, 21-22, 24, 29, 33, 37-38, 43, 48, 56-58, 61-62, 67, 75, 79, 85, 89-91, 97, 100-101, 103, 105, 107-108, 110, 112, 116-120, 124-126, 129, 131

literacy 99-100

literature 105-106, 112-113, 121, 124

logic 22, 31, 39-41, 46, 56

loneliness 107

losses 75, 80, 82, 84

love 13, 15-19, 21-24, 29, 33, 42, 45, 61-62, 64, 70, 75, 90, 105, 112, 129, 131

M

management 40, 55, 68, 109, 117, 119, 121, 124

master's 15, 17-18, 20-21, 24-26, 28, 31, 37-39, 53, 105-106, 111, 116-117, 120-126, 129

meetings 20-21, 27, 68, 116, 130

memories 33, 69, 73, 76, 78-79, 85

mentor 32, 120, 123-124

meritocracy 40

metamorphosis 78

methods 15-16, 19-21, 23, 25-26, 28, 70, 123, 129-130

metrics 62

mind 24, 62, 69, 101

mobilization 40, 78

moment 26, 31, 55, 80, 84, 89, 92, 100, 120-121
multidisciplinary 46
music 66, 85

N

narrative 38-39, 43, 70
neoliberalism 39-40, 46
non-academic 109, 112, 115, 126
non-violent 54
nostalgia 26, 33

O

openness 16, 24, 50, 116, 119
opinion 45, 70
opportunities 20, 52, 93

P

pandemic 17, 73, 75-85, 92, 95, 99-100, 122
paradigms 31, 34, 61-62
participation 19, 26, 40, 43, 52, 65, 98, 111
pedagogy 41, 64-67
perception 105, 108, 112, 115-117, 119-120, 123
performance 100-101, 108, 115
perspective 16, 31, 46, 89, 93, 100, 105-106, 109
PhD 15, 17-18, 20-21, 28, 52, 129
philosophy 50, 55, 64-65, 69
pimping 24
platform 43, 111
pleasure 131
poetry 66
policies 51, 55, 57, 89, 119
politeness 109
possibilities 24, 33, 46, 68, 81, 93, 97, 99-100, 119, 126
power 15, 20, 28, 40, 44, 78, 129
praxis 99-100
preparation 21, 65, 109
prescriptions 23
presence 19, 26, 76
presentation 16, 108, 113
pressure 45, 48, 57
problem 38, 41, 46, 121, 125
productivity 46, 48, 106, 108, 113
profession 91-92, 97, 99
professor 19, 31-32, 44, 93, 99, 106, 120, 129
program 15-19, 32, 37, 39, 44-45, 47-48, 50, 53-57, 79, 90, 105, 111-112, 114, 119-120, 122, 126

project 19, 21, 38, 49, 57, 115, 123

proof   132

proposal   31, 37, 41, 68, 89, 91, 100, 115, 117-118, 120, 123

protagonism   48, 118, 125

protection   82

publication   45, 48, 57

Q

qualification   111, 123

qualitative   39, 43, 49, 105, 110

quality 23, 28, 48, 52, 70, 101, 106, 109, 115, 117-118, 130

quantitative   46, 115

questionnaire   92, 96, 105, 111, 113

R

readings   21, 39, 55, 89, 91, 97, 99-100

reality 31, 46-47, 69, 77-78, 80, 84, 93, 96-97, 99

recognition   52

reflection   31-32, 48, 54, 58, 92, 100-101, 126

relationships   15-16, 22-23, 25, 28, 43, 75-76, 106-109, 121, 124, 126, 129, 131

remote 15, 17, 19-20, 23, 26, 28, 31, 129-130

research   20, 27, 37-38, 43-45, 47-50, 57, 61, 89-92, 94, 96, 99-100, 105-106, 108-113, 115, 117-120, 122-126

researchers   44, 56, 105, 110, 117, 120, 125

resilience   84

resistance   25, 41, 89

resources   96-99

responsibilities 107, 122

retention   51, 57

richness   15, 20-21, 28

role   40, 54, 98-100

routine 121-122

S

sacrifices   106

sadness   81, 131

satisfaction   110, 112, 115, 122-125

scenario   75, 78-79, 84-85, 101

scene   80, 83

scholarship   112

science 35, 37-39, 49, 53, 55-56, 66, 78, 80, 92

self-assessment   110

self-reflection   32

singularities   108

skills   105, 109

society 15, 27, 45, 54-55, 75,

84-85, 131
solidarity   19
speech 48-50, 52, 54, 69, 80, 100-101, 114, 116, 121-122
standpoint   17, 25
strangeness   31, 70
strategies   83, 110
subject 20, 77, 89, 92-93, 98, 109, 113, 124
subjectivities   25, 40, 56, 82, 108
subjects   65, 68, 92, 94, 98, 106
success 41, 57, 109-110
suffering   40, 57, 76, 85
supervisor   103, 106-109, 111, 113-118, 120-123, 126
survey 92, 112

T

teacher 21, 23, 61, 65, 69, 87, 89, 91, 94, 97, 99, 101, 107, 110, 131
teaching   24-25, 27-28, 31, 34, 41, 43-45, 56, 59, 61-62, 64, 67-71, 89, 93, 95, 97-98, 100-101, 107, 109-110, 130
teaching-learning   98, 110
technique   39, 62
technologies   89, 91-93, 95-98, 101
theories   27-28, 50, 61

therapy   48, 53
tools   49-50, 57, 82, 96, 131
topics   22, 43
trajectories   32, 107, 113
transdisciplinary   16, 20, 49, 94, 98
transformations   75-77, 84
translation   40-42, 46, 50, 55, 90-93, 97-99, 119
trauma 123
trust   42
truth   130
tuition   16-17, 130
tuition-free   130

U

UFRJ   15, 17-19, 90
uncertainties   82
undergraduate 15, 17, 25-26, 38, 120
university   15-19, 23-25, 27, 31-32, 37, 39, 44, 49-51, 53, 79, 90, 105, 107, 111, 122, 129

V

values 15, 25, 27, 42-43, 46, 52, 70
violence   23
virtual 32

Index

voices 29, 75, 129

vulnerability 76

W

Waldorf 61-62, 64-70

weaknesses 80, 100

wealth 33, 77

wishes 18, 45

workplace 41

works 27, 49-50, 106, 129

workshop 53

world 24-25, 32-33, 40, 42, 62, 70, 77, 80, 85, 91, 93, 100

wounds 75

Y

youth 84

About the authors

Ana Paula André

Master in Literature from the State University of Western Paraná (UNIOESTE), Cascavel Campus. Specialist in Fundamentals of Education from UNIOESTE. Specialist in Youth and Adult Education from ESAB. Specialist in Special Education from FAVED. Graduated in Pedagogy from UNIOESTE. Works as a pedagogue in Basic Education at the State Department of Education of Paraná. She has experience in teaching Early Childhood Education and Elementary Education, as a pedagogical coordinator in Youth and Adult Education, Elementary Education and High School. Member of the Study and Research Group on Social Education and Youth and Adult Education (GEPESEJA), at UFSCAR in Sorocaba, São Paulo, Brazil.

Orcid: https://orcid.org/0000-0003-3374-8333

E-mail: aninhandre21@gmail.com

Cláucia Piccoli Faganello

Curious by nature, I have always believed that I don't know enough and I need to learn more. This was the question that led me here and encouraged me to pursue academia. But not a resigned academic life, a questioning one. Studying, sharing with other people and traveling are my great passions. There are also cats, these incredible and wise beings that teach me so much about how to live and accompany me in reading and writing.

I was born in the interior of Rio Grande do Sul, Brazil, in Veranópolis, in the Serra Gaúcha region, but I always knew I wouldn't stay there. I graduated in Administration: Public Management (UERGS) and Law (UniRitter), specialized in Municipal Public Management (UFRGS), did my master's degree in Sociology (UFRGS) and am currently studying for a PhD in Administration (PUCRS).

Anyone who wants to exchange experiences and build bridges can contact me via email: claucia.f@gmail.com

Igor Vinicius Lima Valentim

I was born in Rio de Janeiro, Brazil, and have always loved living an almost nomadic life. People's stories fascinate me. I have lived in places such as Porto Alegre, Balneário Camboriú, Itajaí, Criciúma, Ribeirão Preto, Itapiranga, Lisbon (Portugal) and on the island of São Miguel, in the middle of the Atlantic Ocean, in the Azores archipelago. I currently work as a professor at the Federal University of Rio de Janeiro (UFRJ) and in the Graduate Program in History of Sciences and Techniques and Epistemology, at UFRJ itself.

I love controversial and polemic topics that are thrown under the carpet or left behind the scenes. Some subjects I have discussed: academic pimping, power, curiosity, qualitative research, autoethnography, cartography, active learning, education, university, transdisciplinarity, subjectivity and trust.

You can also find me on the Youtube channel **Experiências e Epifanias** or by e-mail: valentim@gmail.com

Previously, I have written When money is not above everything: other ways of working, generating income, and living and some other books in Portuguese: Residência Solidária UFRGS: vivência de universitários com o desenvolvimento de uma tecnologia social (Editora da UFRGS); Economia Solidária em Portugal: inspirações cartográficas; Metodologias ativas no ensino remoto: uma autoetnografia; Cafetinagem acadêmica, assédio moral e autoetnografia; and Desafios e estratégias na Pós-Graduação: uma conversa necessária (Editora Compassos Coletivos).

Kelly Cebelia das Chagas do Amaral

Born in the spring of 1979, her name was Kelly Cristina, but her mother had met a very naughty child with that name, so she decided to change Cristina to Cebelia... I confess that I liked it!

Raised in the countryside of the Amazon, she had the dream of being a dancer, and then a flight attendant. The reality was better than the dream, she graduated in Physical Education from the Federal University of Acre. So, she can teach dance classes, gymnastics, sports, recreation and everything else she wants. She is currently carrying out her PhD research in Education at the State University of Londrina, traveling Brazil and Argentina in search of schools that reinvent themselves and adopt teaching practices that are different from conventional ones.

Najara Escarião Agripino

Master's and Bachelor's degrees in Administration; Specialist in Human Resources, Labor Routines and Calculations. She is currently a graduate student in International Relations and a research member in the research groups Environment, Tourism and Sustainability Research Group – GEATS; and Research in Political Communication, Media and Elections. In Administration, she researches Sustainability, Education and Organizational Learning. In International Relations she researches China on the topics of Ecological Civilization, Orientalism and Soft Power.

Paulo de Tarso Xavier Sousa Junior

Graduated in Psychology from Centro Universitário UniFacid | Wyden. Master's in Psychology from the Federal University of Santa Maria (UFSM). Research Assistant at Fiocruz Piauí. Professor at the State University of Maranhão (UEMA).

www.ingramcontent.com/pod-product-compliance
Lightning Source LLC
LaVergne TN
LVHW041607070526
838199LV00052B/3024